A DARK HISTORY:
THE ROMAN
EMPERORS

A DARK HISTORY:
THE ROMAN
EMPERORS

FROM JULIUS CAESAR TO THE FALL OF ROME

MICHAEL KERRIGAN

METRO BOOKS
NEW YORK

Metro Books
122 Fifth Avenue
New York, NY 10011

Editorial and design by
Amber Books Ltd

Project Editor: James Bennett
Designer: Colin Hawes
Picture Research: Terry Forshaw, Kate Green

ISBN: 978-1-4351-3277-1

Printed and bound in China

1   3   5   7   9   10   8   6   4   2

CONTENTS

PROLOGUE

Assassination, incest, intrigue, corruption … For all its unrivalled achievements and surpassing splendour, there was an infinitely darker side to ancient Rome. Nowhere were the stakes higher, the passions fiercer or the politicking more murderous than they were at the very top, in the imperial court.

◆

rash! The hall fell silent at the noise, and for an instant everybody froze. They glanced across to where the slave stood quaking. Before him on the floor lay the silver salver of food he had dropped. He was destined for a flogging, they all thought, especially because he had been at work up on the central dais where the imperial family was served. The Emperor was not going to be amused.

And then, just beyond him, they saw just what it was that had startled the slave so much. Bolt upright,

Left: The Roman Forum was very much a public space. Like the Athenian agora, it had originally been a place for meeting and for democratic discussion of affairs. These republican ideals were consigned firmly to the past, however, with the rise of Rome's first Emperor, Augustus (above).

his body rigid, young Britannicus sat there, the terror of death in eyes that looked frantically before him yet didn't seem to see. The boy's face, ghostly pale, was contorted into an unnatural grimace. He appeared to be trying to speak, but could only gasp.

The Emperor's guests stood up now and moved forwards hesitantly. They should help, they thought, but dared they approach the couches where the Emperor's closest relatives were? They, too, seemed stunned, sitting up on the couches where moments earlier they had been reclining at their ease, gaping helplessly at the Emperor's stricken stepbrother.

Only the Emperor himself seemed calm, and master of the situation. He quickly took charge. Britannicus had always been prone to such seizures, he explained. There was absolutely no cause for concern. They should continue with their meal, he insisted. The young man would recover in no time. And so, reassured, they did: a little uncertainly, at first, and then more happily by degrees. The fare was sumptuous; the wine was good, and it was flowing freely. The murmur of conversation rose, and soon the incident had been all but forgotten. The imperial banquet was once more in full swing.

Up on the dais where the first family sat, more complex emotions reigned, as slaves flocked round the boy, who was now slumping limply. With mounting horror, his relatives realized that the Emperor's optimism had been misplaced. This had been no epileptic fit. Britannicus, just a few days before his fourteenth birthday, was dead, struck down by some terrible tragedy.

> The boy's face, ghostly pale, was contorted into an unnatural grimace. He appeared to be trying to speak, but could only gasp.

The fact didn't seem to have registered with the Emperor himself: he still smiled blandly as if nothing very much was wrong. What a shock it would be for him when he was made to understand what had happened. They wondered if they should say something, but nobody dared to be the bringer of bad news.

One woman knew differently, though; she knew the real meaning of Nero's smile. Agrippina, the Emperor's mother, sat on the couch opposite her son, consumed with speechless fury. She had committed her share of murders and knew a poisoning when she saw one. And no one knew the Emperor Nero as well as she did. Britannicus had been a potential rival for the throne. The thought had crossed Agrippina's own mind of assassinating Nero and installing him instead. Her son had rebelled against her and would no longer accept

Rome's republican principles had periodically been tested by attempted coups. Here the great orator Cicero denounces would-be dictator Catiline before the Senate in 63 B.C.E. As time went on, unfortunately, rhetorical eloquence such as Cicero's was no longer going to be an adequate defence for ancient freedoms.

her direction: Britannicus would have been much easier to manipulate.

As she turned it over in her thoughts, her rage became increasingly tinged with fear: with Britannicus gone, who else might seem to threaten Nero's throne? She herself was the obvious person. She would be the Emperor's next target, but how and where would he strike, and exactly when?

BEFORE THE EMPERORS

There weren't supposed to be emperors in Rome. For the first 480 years of its history, Rome's citizens had ruled the city on the Tiber. A republic and proud of it, Rome had come into being in 510 B.C.E., when a group of tribes had banded together to drive out the Etruscan kings. Based in Etruria, to the north, the Etruscans had extended their rule over central Italy, dominating the peoples they found there. The Latins had resented this and, once they had succeeded in freeing themselves, they had resolved to build their own city and their own state, where they would not have to bow to anyone.

Not even to each other: the Romans would conduct the business of state together in a ruling council, which

---

Rome's legions, many hundreds of thousands strong, were feared by every nation in the region, but they were also becoming a threat to Rome itself.

---

they called the Senate. Only the patricians, of course – those representing the leading families – would be members of the Senate. The idea that ordinary men should have a voice would have seemed strange. (The notion that women might speak would have been utterly unthinkable. Every man was supposed to be the master in his own home.)

Rome's republican system worked. The city prospered and the state of Rome grew in power and influence. Soon it had conquered several nearby cities. As the decades and then the centuries passed, it extended its reach across the whole of Italy, and then into other countries around. Between the third and second centuries B.C.E., it fought a series of wars with Carthage, a naval power on the coast of North Africa. In 146 B.C.E., Carthage was at last destroyed, and the Romans ruled the entire Mediterranean basin.

THE STRONGMEN

The Empire kept on growing and extended into the Balkans and the Middle East. Rome's legions, many hundreds of thousands strong, were feared by every nation in the region, but they were also becoming a threat to Rome itself. The great generals were respected, almost revered, by their men, and they could command the loyalty of huge forces. As the Empire grew vaster and more unwieldy, it became harder for the Senate to keep control. If a general didn't want to obey the edicts of the Senate, and his troops supported him, what could the Senate do?

In 88 B.C.E., Lucius Cornelius Sulla was given command of a campaign in what is now Turkey, where King Mithridates VI of Pontus had risen up in rebellion against the power of Rome. The commission was a privilege and also a ticket to considerable wealth because a victorious general could expect to come home with a great deal of booty. So enticing was this particular prize that another general, Gaius Marius, bribed the people's representatives to give him command in Sulla's place.

Sulla, who had just set out for the east, turned in his tracks when he heard the news and marched back with his men. Instead of attacking Pontus, he attacked Rome. Marius' supporters fought back, and there were several days and nights of intense fighting in the streets before Sulla succeeded in gaining the upper hand. Marius fled to North Africa to lick his wounds, while Sulla set off again to deal with Mithridates.

He had hardly turned his back before Marius returned with his friend Lucius Cornelius Cinna. They murdered Sulla's supporters and set themselves up in power in Rome. Marius, however, died of a brain haemorrhage a few weeks later, so never really had time to enjoy the triumphs of his devious plot. Cinna was sitting pretty – that is, until the reports started coming in that Sulla was on his way home. At

Right: Sulla seized dictatorial power for himself in 81 B.C.E. and quickly set about liquidating his opponents. But even he had the humility to step down of his own accord once he had made his point: it never occurred to him to set himself up as emperor.

SPARTACUS AND THE SLAVES

Spartacus came from Thrace, in the north of Greece, and had been an auxiliary soldier with the Roman army there, before falling foul of the law for desertion and robbery. For these crimes, he was condemned to be a gladiator, and to fight with others in the public arena. He would have a violent, bloody life, and almost certainly a short one. Spartacus was completing his gladiatorial training with 70 other unfortunates when he managed to persuade them to mutiny with him. Using stolen kitchen knives and cleavers, they managed to force their way out and escaped into the hills above the Bay of Naples.

There they lived as outlaws, gathering more and more recruits as runaway slaves came and asked to join them. There were hundreds of them by the time a Roman army was sent out to deal with them. Spartacus quickly outwitted the Romans and defeated them in a surprise attack. News of this improbable victory spread far and wide through Italy; slaves escaped by the thousands and flocked to follow Spartacus. Eventually, he had more than 120,000 troops at his command, trained up by his gladiator friends. The troops were also desperate, with nothing to lose because they knew capture would mean a cruel death.

Spartacus' outlaw slaves won a series of victories, before Marcus Licinius Crassus came with a huge army and managed to corner them in Calabria, the 'toe' of Italy. Although Spartacus, a general of genius, succeeded against all the odds in breaking out, he found himself facing another vast army. Gnaeus Pompeius Magnum, who was already known as Pompey the Great for his victories in war, led this one.

Those of Spartacus' men who were cut down by the advancing legions were the lucky ones. Those who were captured (6000 in all) were crucified at intervals up and down the Appian Way, the main road to Rome. Nailed alive onto crosses of wood, they died a lingering, unspeakably agonizing death. Their bodies were then left hanging there, picked at by crows until the flesh hung in tatters, then slowly decaying over weeks and months. Ultimately, the macabre crucifixes with their skeletons were to remain by the roadside for many years, a clear warning to any slave who passed.

Kirk Douglas took the role of the rebel slave Spartacus in Stanley Kubrick's 1960 movie of the same name. Sir Laurence Olivier played his nemesis, Marcus Licinius Crassus.

that point, Cinna was killed by his own troops, who did not want to find themselves on the wrong side of Sulla when he returned.

Marius had been survived by a number of his henchmen, though, and they were by no means eager to surrender power. Determined to make a fight of it, they resisted doggedly, and Sulla made it back to Rome only after 18 months of bitter civil war.

SULLA IN POWER

Re-entering his capital, Sulla was in no mood to see it taken from him again. In 81 B.C.E., the Senate elected him dictator. That was pretty much the last thing they were allowed to do because from that time onwards Sulla's word was law. In the meantime, his supporters rooted out anyone suspected of having collaborated with the previous regime. This included those who might be seen as a threat to Sulla's power, even if they had not collaborated. Hundreds were proscribed (denounced as enemies of the state). More than 1500 patricians were executed. Many committed suicide. Rather than leave themselves to the mercy of Sulla's men, they preferred to run themselves through with their own swords or slit their wrists. This had the advantage that, under Roman law, their wealth and possessions would remain with their families. If you were killed as a traitor your goods went to the state, which, in this case, was Sulla.

But the bloodletting extended far beyond the patrician class. Anyone associated with a proscribed person was condemned with them as far as Sulla was concerned. Helping a traitor, or even showing sympathy with his plight, was an act of treason in itself. A mood of paranoia developed and, by the time the panic had run its course, more than 9000 people had lost their lives. Even so, in these comparatively innocent times, Rome's default position was democratic. After two years in power, Sulla resigned voluntarily from his dictatorship.

JULIUS CAESAR

Among those forced to flee Rome at the time of Sulla's purges was the young Julius Caesar. As the nephew of Marius, he was a marked man. To make matters worse, he had married Cinna's daughter, and he refused to divorce her when her father was proscribed. Stripped of his rank and possessions, Caesar had to go into hiding.

Caesar's mother had connections in Sulla's circle, and in time they were able to smooth things over sufficiently for the death sentence hanging over him to be lifted. But Sulla was still suspicious, which made Rome an uncomfortable place. So, Caesar took himself off to join the army, where he made his name as a brave and intelligent young officer. By the time Sulla died in 78 B.C.E., Caesar was a man on the rise.

Back in Rome, he began cementing his reputation. A brilliant speaker and a skilled politician, he quickly made up the lost time of the Sulla years. A successful campaign of conquest in Spain made him a hero to his

> Helping a traitor, or even showing sympathy with his plight, was an act of treason in itself. A mood of paranoia developed and, by the time the panic had run its course, more than 9000 people had lost their lives.

legions, giving him military muscle to back the personal aura he already had. Like many generals throughout history, Caesar was impatient with the dithering of the politicians back home and started to wonder why he should be at the Senate's beck and call. He soon found that other successful generals of the day were thinking along the same lines, especially Crassus and Pompey, who were fresh from their triumph over Spartacus' rebellion.

Together, they formed a triumvirate (literally, government by three men). Its official status was ambiguous, at least at first. In theory, the trio was wielding power on behalf of a supportive Senate, but it was hard to see what choice the Senate had. Pompey had parked his legions outside the capital as a discreet reminder of the force he could always summon up if needed. Where representatives failed to take the hint, his men were more direct. One senator, Bibulus, who tried Caesar's patience a little too far with his outspoken opposition, received his lesson when a group of thugs emptied a bucket of excrement over his head. In the circumstances, few felt inclined to continue resistance to what we would now call a general's coup.

A FAIR PRICE

Julius Caesar was never short of self-esteem. He quickly became famous in Rome as a thrilling public speaker. When he was making a journey to Rhodes in the Greek islands to study with a famous teacher of oratory in 75 B.C.E., however, he was captured by Cicilian pirates and put up for ransom. Told by his captors that they were charging 20 golden talents for his release, he reacted with indignation and insisted that they demand 50. From the start to the finish of his imprisonment, he carried himself with a disdainful dignity. He was never in awe of those who had such power over him.

When the money was paid and Caesar set free, he promised to come back to find the pirates and bring them to justice. They laughed, assuming that he meant this as a joke. On the contrary, Caesar quickly called a fleet together and set to sea; in no time he had caught the pirates and taken them to the shores of Asia Minor (modern Turkey) and presented them to the Roman governor there. To his outrage, the official was not interested in making a public example of the pirates, preferring to have the money he could earn by selling them as slaves. Caesar promptly took his prisoners back, marched them down to the coast where they would be seen from passing ships and, on his own authority, crucified them there and then.

He was not destined to be Emperor himself, but the office is inconceivable without him: Julius Caesar had both the imperial vision and the ego to go with it. Ironically, the conspirators who killed him almost certainly only hastened the end of the republic they were trying to save.

CONQUERING HERO

Being one among three, even at the head of the greatest empire the world had ever seen, was never going to satisfy Caesar for long. Far from plotting against his partners in government, though, he made a point of throwing himself into the patriotic task of making the Roman Empire even greater. During the 50s B.C.E., he and his legions conquered the vast territory of Gaul, modern France, and made exploratory forays into Germany and Britain. If he displayed to the full his dazzling generalship, Caesar showed his sheer ruthlessness as well, carrying out massacres among rebellious populations. A million

In 60 B.C.E., Pompey had the Roman world at his feet – or at least a third of it, as a member of the Triumvirate with Julius Caesar and Marcus Licinius Crassus. It was not to last: there was no stopping Caesar's rise to supreme authority in Rome.

people were killed. This is a truly staggering figure when you set it against the fact that the total population for the country was somewhere around four million.

When one township, Avaricum (Bourges), refused to give in, Caesar had his men dig in for an extended siege. The inhabitants' courage only infuriated Caesar. In the event, when the town was taken after 25 days, his troops put its people systematically to the sword. Only 800 escaped. A horrifying 40,000 were exterminated, serving as an example for any other rebellious Gauls.

> To go further would be an act of war but, for Caesar, retreat was unthinkable. '*Alea iacta est* (The die is cast),' he said, giving the order to go on.

Back home, people were, of course, sheltered from the realities of the Gallic killing fields, and Caesar was seen entirely in heroic terms. As surely as his popular adulation soared, however, his popularity with his partners in the Triumvirate plummeted. Pompey in particular felt threatened. He made the Senate order Caesar to stand his army down. When Caesar failed to do so, he was charged with treason against the state.

Like Sulla before him, Caesar now found himself at odds with his own empire. From his base in Gaul, he headed southwards with his legion. Soon they were standing on the banks of the River Rubicon, at the frontier of Italy itself. To go further would be an act of war but for Caesar, retreat was unthinkable. '*Alea iacta est* (The die is cast),' he said, giving the order to go on. Having crossed the Rubicon, Caesar was officially an enemy of the state. The civil war he had started was to last two years.

CAESAR'S CIVIL WAR

Pompey appears to have been taken aback by the speed and resolution of Caesar's attack. Although his forces far outnumbered Caesar's, Pompey did not stand and fight. Instead, commandeering every ship he could, he evacuated some to Greece and some to Spain, and prepared for a lengthy, empire-wide campaign.

Caesar, however, was not to be resisted. He established his friend Marcus Antonius (also called Mark Antony) as his tribune in Rome itself. He then marched his army overland all the way to Spain, completing the journey in an incredible 27 days. Pompey's forces there were not at all ready for his arrival and, in the absence of Pompey himself, they were easily defeated. Caesar now turned and headed eastwards back through Gaul and across Italy to where Pompey was securing his powerbase in Greece. Caesar's exhausted, overstretched army was a hair's breadth from defeat when it met Pompey's fresh forces at the Battle of Dyrrhachium on 10 January in 48 B.C.E. Back in Rome, Caesar was named as dictator, but he made a point of relinquishing this title, amid great publicity, a few days later.

EGYPTIAN DIVERSIONS

Pompey, meanwhile, had fled to Alexandria in Egypt, hoping for the protection of the local king Ptolemy XIII. Caesar came in pursuit, but Pompey had been executed by the time he arrived. Ptolemy had ordered the deed, apparently in hopes of pleasing Rome. Two Romans, old soldiers of Pompey's but now in Ptolemy's service, had been sent out in a boat to welcome Pompey's vessel into port. They offered to take Pompey ashore for an audience with the Egyptian ruler, who had promised to take him in. The boat was heading for the shore with Pompey and his family. The Roman general was working on his speech of gratitude to Ptolemy when his former comrades suddenly stabbed him in the back before his terrified wife and children could react.

Ptolemy had the body beheaded and presented to Julius Caesar on his arrival, but the dictator turned out to be anything but pleased. He chose to see the ill treatment of Pompey as an outrageous slight to Rome, and lent his support to Ptolemy's enemies in what was brewing up to be an Egyptian civil war. By a long-standing tradition, Ptolemy XIII was married to his

Julius Caesar crosses the Rubicon, as imagined by the monkish artist of this illuminated manuscript of the fifteenth century. The moment was symbolic, as it represented Caesar's defiance of the law as laid down by the Senate – his clear hint that he was his own authority.

Er commance lucan en suiuant sa ma
tiere de Cesar son second liure et deuise com
ment cesar et ses legions partirent de Rauenne
et sen vindrent sur le fleuue de Rubicon [.]

Uant Cesar qui adoncques estoit
en Rauenne a tout son ost eur la
nouuelle que le senat auoit
refusee la requeste que les tri
buns faisoient pour lui Et que les tribuns
estoient .oooooooo. departiz par de la Cite
de Romme Il fist tantost appareiller toutes
ses legions et les ennoia tout couuuent de
la Cite de Rauenne que les citoiens ne appar
ceussent que il voulsist ennair Romme et son
deuise Car espoir silz le sceussent ilz le voul
sissent retenir et prendre comme ceulx qui
estoient de la puissance de Romme Et pour

mieulx faindre la chose Il ala auecques les Ci
toiens au teatre pour regarder les commune
veu de la ville Et ala regardant vne grant
place ou il deuoit faire edifier vne cercle ou
les cheualliers aue espees se combatoient en
la guise qui est deuise ca arriere Et puis ala
Cesar souper si comme il auoit accoustume quant
il et fait appareiller richement son cure de les
vui jour et vn reffin qui estoit de les son hostel
et furent les milles bien dong au cure et bien
atelle Il monta sur et sen yssi de la ville par
vui reffort sentier a tout vni decomunune
et eira tant apres que chandelles furent eftautes
quel il trouua vni fleuue vers le jour par qui
enseignement Il fut auoie et aui se su emba
tu en vn destour dont Il commut que Il et les
siens yssissent tout apres ny auoit point de

Pompey's assassination suited Caesar, just as Egypt's King Ptolemy had guessed it would, but he chose to take offence at the slight to Rome. For all his upfront arrogance and audacity, Caesar could scheme with the best of them: it was dangerous to underestimate his low cunning.

sister Cleopatra. In name, at least, she was his co-ruler. But she was determined to reign in her own right. Cleopatra took advantage of Caesar's arrival by getting him to back her in what became a civil war. In 47 B.C.E., Caesar's troops won the Battle of the Nile, and Cleopatra became queen of Egypt, as well as a loyal client of Rome.

GENERAL, DICTATOR ... KING?

When Caesar returned to Rome, his popularity was sky-high. He bestowed lavish shows and games to celebrate his victories. That kept the people on his side, although they already adored him as the conqueror of Gaul. He was shrewd in his handling of the patrician class as well. Caesar had already shown in Gaul that he could be ruthless when the situation required it, and there is no doubt that he could be politically ruthless, too.

Much as he himself had suffered at Sulla's hands, Caesar had been withering in his scorn when he heard of his resignation. Sulla had been a fool, he said, to surrender his power so lightly. Now, though, Caesar refused to proscribe any of his opponents. As a result, even those who didn't share his views regarded him with respect and gratitude.

It was too good to last. Caesar was once more given the title of Dictator, and this time he did not renounce it 10 days later. As Caesar-mania continued to surge, however, and people started talking about having him crowned king, members of the nobility began to grow concerned. Caesar had already talked about bequeathing his dictator's title to his great-nephew and adopted son Gaius Julius Caesar Octavianus (Octavian) after his death. But did Rome really want to be under the authority of another dynasty of kings?

CONSPIRACY

The disgruntled nobles clustered around the figure of Marcus Junius Brutus, a member of one of Rome's most distinguished families. Brutus had been one of Caesar's closest friends, and an invaluable ally in the war with Pompey, but he viewed the current situation with alarm. If Caesar's rise were to go unchecked, what would become of all the liberties for which Rome's founders had fought so hard in centuries past? Proud of his ancient ancestors who had helped to rid the early Romans of the Etruscan tyrants, Brutus regularly visited their marble busts to pay them respect. More and more frequently, though, he found them marked with anonymous graffiti asking how the descendant of such heroes could be standing meekly by while a new tyranny was being built.

Brutus was stirred to action and, with a man of his stature taking a lead, what had been vague mutterings crystallized into a serious conspiracy. Brutus' brother-in-law Cassius seems actually to have been the man who hatched the plot. Brutus was brave and idealistic,

---

As Caesar-mania continued to surge, however, and people started talking about having him crowned king, members of the nobility began to grow concerned.

---

but too openly honest to take charge of a business such as this. They were going to have to be ruthless. Caesar would never allow himself to be shamed or bullied into standing down. They knew it had to be assassination or nothing. The conspirators resolved to make their move on the Ides (the fifteenth day) of March, 44 B.C.E. As the time approached, their apprehensions rose. There was an atmosphere of foreboding around the city. One day, on leaving the Senate building, Julius Caesar was stopped by a soothsayer who warned him grimly – if cryptically – 'Beware the Ides of March!' Meanwhile, Caesar's wife Calpurnia had a dream in which she saw her husband's statue with its lifeblood gushing out from a thousand places. Caesar scoffed: the conqueror of Gaul and vanquisher of Pompey was not going to be fazed by a woman's fears.

'ET TU, BRUTE ...?'

When the day came, events unfolded rapidly and every bit as excitingly as they do in Shakespeare's famous drama, *Julius Caesar*. The conspirators were only seconds away from everything going completely wrong. Servilius Casca, in his anxiety, on the eve of the attack

CAESAR AND CLEOPATRA

Cleopatra was 21 when she first met Julius Caesar, and by all accounts she was a stunning beauty. By Roman standards, she was utterly exotic with her dark skin, her rich jewels and her sumptuously dressed hair. She was openly attracted to the 51-year-old Julius Caesar, and especially to his power.

Famously, she had herself smuggled into his presence rolled up inside a richly woven carpet. It was sent as a gift, but when it was unrolled before the Roman she emerged and offered herself to him. Their affair was eventually to go on for more than a decade, and they even had a son, Caesarion. The laws of Rome did not allow Caesar to marry Cleopatra because she was an alien. Strangely, though, as they did not recognize the relationship at all in legal terms, the laws did not class it as adultery. Not only did Caesar continue his affair with Cleopatra throughout his time in Egypt, but she also came to visit him several times subsequently in Rome. On and off, the affair lasted 14 years, during all of which time Caesar was married to his third wife, Calpurnia Pisonis.

Cleopatra brought a powerful note of exoticism – and eroticism – to Roman history. Her legendary looks played political havoc in the affairs of the late Roman Republic.

Previous page: Brutus, as imagined by Michelangelo amidst the republican resurgence of the Renaissance. The medieval poet Dante had damned Brutus to the deepest pit of hell for rebelling against authority. Brutus had seen himself as standing up for Rome's highest traditions, though his noble crime was to have ignoble consequences.

had let slip a remark in front of Mark Antony, Caesar's most trusted friend. While the comment did not betray the plot exactly, it aroused Antony's suspicions. He was on his way to the Senate to intercept Caesar and warn him when Caesar left the building and was approached by Tillius Cimber, who asked Caesar to read a petition he had brought.

The document was a fake – but it was good enough to hold up and distract Caesar for as long as it took for Cimber to grab his tunic. At that point, Casca struck Caesar's neck a glancing blow with his dagger. After this, the blows came raining in, in such a storm that the assassins several times nicked each other, but more than 20 blows struck Caesar himself. Traditionally, though, the blow that killed him came from the man he had thought was his friend. '*Et tu, Brute...?*' ('You too, Brutus...?') he said, whereupon he died.

'CRY "HAVOC!"

The conspirators consoled one another by saying that what they had been forced to do was sad, but necessary. The Republic had been threatened, but they had saved it. Yet the reality was that, with their daggers, they had done to death not just Julius Caesar, but the republican ideal as well. In the atmosphere of anger, fear and paranoia that resulted from the assassination, there was no prospect of Romans being able to work together in a common cause.

Undaunted by the warnings, Julius Caesar makes his way to the Senate on the Ides of March, 44 B.C.E. Caesar's story haunted the French artists of the post-revolutionary period: Alexandre-Denis Abel de Pujol (1787–1861) was to return to it several times.

DAY OF DESTINY

'Beware the Ides of March!' the soothsayer is supposed to have said to Caesar as he left the Senate one day. The fateful day was the fifteenth of the month. In the old, lunar calendar, the Ides had been the date of the full moon, but by now it was just a convenient division, halfway through the month.

Even if the 'Ides of March' hadn't become famous as a general sort of day of doom, and even if Julius Caesar hadn't been well known for any other reason, he would still have had his place in history as the inaugurator of the 'Julian calendar', which rationalized what had, until then, been a haphazard system for keeping track of the passing of time. Previously, the Roman calendar was made up of 12 months, coming to a total of 355 days. This had gradually fallen out of synch with the rhythms of the solar year, so an extra month had been periodically inserted between February and March. This 'Mensis Intercalaris' had 27 days, and it took up the slack in the old system to a certain point. But even so the calendar year had parted company with the cycle of the seasons, with their solstices and equinoxes.

The Julian calendar was a vast improvement: it had 365 days, like our own. Year on year, it was as close to correct as made no difference. But the old system had gone so badly wrong that, for its first of January to start at a sensible point in the solar cycle, it had to be preceded by a special year 445 days long. So what we would call 46 B.C.E. (the Romans saw it as the 709th year since their city's founding) lasted well into what should have been 45 B.C.E.

Once it was up and running, the new system worked far better. The priests who worked it out had realized the need for 'leap' years to keep the cycle on track, but they miscalculated and had them at three-yearly intervals. Even so, it didn't do badly: only very gradually did its slight inaccuracies add up to a more significant cumulative error. By the sixteenth century, though, the Julian calendar was 10 days astray. At that point, Pope Gregory XIII introduced a new 'Gregorian' calendar.

The Death of Caesar by **Vincenzo Camuccini (1771–1884), captures all the drama of an assassination, the importance of which has resonated into the modern age. For the Romans, the rights and wrongs of the matter all too quickly became irrelevant as the Empire spiralled into civil war.**

Hypocrisy was the order of the day. Mark Antony adopted a conciliatory manner with the conspirators while secretly planning to get his friend's revenge. In a speech immortalized by Shakespeare ('Friends, Romans, countrymen ...'), he addressed the crowd at Caesar's funeral, whipping it up into a fury against Brutus and his crew.

The conspirators were forced to flee to Greece, but as soon as they arrived they started making preparations to return in force. Brutus had a power base among the legions of southeastern Europe and Asian Minor. Against them, however, Mark Antony and Octavian, Caesar's adopted son and appointed heir, were raising their own army with the help of Lepidus, another friend of Caesar's. The Senate officially recognized the three men as the Second Triumvirate, the official rulers of the Roman state. The Second Triumvirate had the Senate acknowledge the late Julius Caesar as a god to underline the propaganda point that their cause was just. It also had the consequence that, as *Divi Filius* ('son of god'), Octavian could claim to be ruling by divine right.

> Antony and Cleopatra, in addition to being passionate lovers, were setting themselves up as a 'power couple' bent on building their own empire in the east.

They led their army out to meet Brutus' force, which was even now advancing on Rome. The two sides met at Philippi, in Macedonia. On 3 October 42 B.C.E., the First Battle of Philippi was fought. Brutus' troops engaged those of Octavian, and seemed to be on the verge of victory. At the same time, however, Cassius' army was coming off badly against Antony's. In the moment of defeat, unaware that Brutus' wing had fared far better, Cassius had his friend and freedman Pindarus run him through with his sword.

Brutus' force was weakened, and he was in no hurry to renew the attack. He had high hopes of his ships, currently fighting the Triumvirate's fleet at sea. If they did as much damage as he expected, his army would not have to renew the fight at all. His enemies would have been left stranded, high and dry, without ships or supplies. The strategy might have worked had his troops on shore not grown restless and impatient. Soon they were beginning to desert his army. Brutus was pretty much compelled to attack his enemy while he still had an army to do it with, but his situation was less than ideal and it quickly showed. His men were quickly forced into a retreat and, with all now evidently lost, Brutus, too, committed suicide rather than fall into the hands of his enemies.

THREE'S A CROWD

When a man has come close to supreme power, why would he be interested in sharing it? In the end, the Second Triumvirate was to go the way of the first, and for the same reasons. Not that there wasn't plenty of Empire to go round. Octavian ruled the west, from Rome; Antony ruled the east, from Alexandria; and Lepidus was allotted the rest of North Africa.

Lepidus had been the weakest of the trio from the beginning, although for a while he had a role as mediator between the mutually suspicious Octavian and Antony. They had never been natural allies, even if their shared desire to avenge Caesar (and gain power at his assassins' expense) had brought them together for a while. When, in 43 B.C.E., Lepidus attempted to boost his authority by helping himself to some of Octavian's legions, Octavian had him expelled from the Triumvirate. This meant more territory for both Octavian and Antony; however, without Lepidus to deal between them, their rivalry only grew.

CLEOPATRA, AGAIN

Octavian's feelings towards Antony had not become any warmer since the revelation that, now that he was installed in Alexandria, Antony had taken up with Caesar's sometime mistress Cleopatra. Antony and Cleopatra, in addition to being passionate lovers, were setting themselves up as a 'power couple' bent on building their own empire in the east.

As Octavian's anger seethed, Antony began to wonder if he might not have gone too far. In 40 B.C.E., he ended his relationship with Cleopatra and tried to make things up with his co-ruler in Rome. So successfully were they

Right: Mark Antony and Cleopatra lead a carefree life of love and idle revelry in this 1717 painting by Francesco Trevisani. They were living on borrowed time: by 31 B.C.E., Octavian had massed his forces against them, and their romantic idyll ended in tragedy.

BLOOD PROPHECY

Shakespeare caught to perfection the mood of Mark Antony, who was forced to speak softly to the killers of his friend. His words over Caesar's body were uttered in the manner of a prophecy. He was to do his best to make sure that the prediction was fulfilled.

> *Oh pardon me thou bleeding piece of earth*
> *That I am meek and gentle with these butchers!*
> *Thou are the ruins of the noblest man*
> *That ever lived in the tide of times:*
> *Woe to the hand that shed this costly blood!*
> *Over thy wounds now do I prophesy…*
> *A curse shall light upon the affairs of men.*
> *Domestic fury and fierce civil strife*
> *Shall cumber all the parts of Italy.*
> *Blood and destruction shall be so in use,*
> *And dreadful objects so familiar,*
> *That mothers shall but smile when they behold*
> *Their infants quartered with the hands of war;*
> *All pity choked with custom of fell deeds.*
> *And Caesar's spirit, ranging for revenge,*
> *With Ate by his side, come hot from hell,*
> *Shall in these confines, with a monarch's voice,*
> *Cry 'Havoc!' and let slip the dogs of war …*

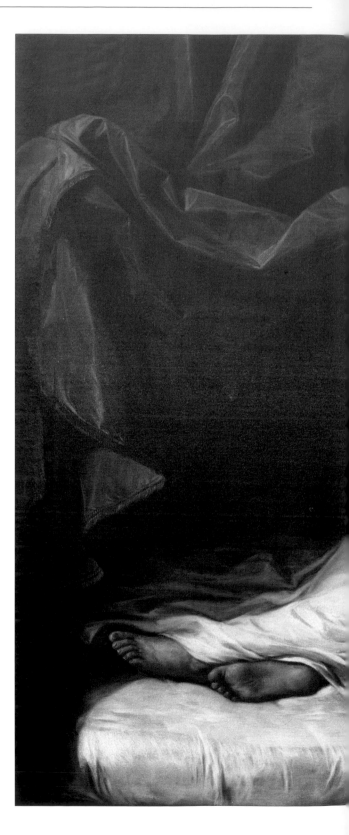

A pin-up to posterity, Cleopatra's image has proved particularly haunting in the moment of her tragic death in 30 B.C.E. The Egyptian queen was actually rather less romantic than she seemed. She was in fact a shrewd manipulator of men and a resourceful and ruthless political operator.

reconciled that Octavian sealed their friendship by giving Antony the hand of his sister, Octavia, in marriage.

This, of course, only made it worse when, just three years later, Antony left Rome (and Octavia) for Alexandria, where he took up with Cleopatra again.

TO THE VICTOR, THE SPOILS

Octavian wasn't sentimental, although as a Roman man he felt keenly the loss of face his family had suffered as a result of Antony's behaviour. Such personal resentments apart, there was also the simple

fact that, ever since Lepidus' dismissal, the balance of power in the Empire had been delicately poised. However sincerely Octavian and Antony may have meant their reconciliation, eventual conflict between them was inevitable. The potential was clear for the winner to take all in a civil war.

EGYPT DEFEATED AT SEA

Civil war is precisely what followed. Octavian began spreading stories against Antony in Rome, implying that he was 'going native' in Egypt with his exotic queen. Soon he felt confident enough to send a war fleet against Egypt: the fleet met with Cleopatra's ships off the coast of Greece. The Battle of Actium (2 September

---

In 27 B.C.E., though, they gave Octavian the honorific name, Augustus ('splendid') … No one had formally proclaimed him Emperor, as such. Although he was seems to have grown into an emperor by slow degrees in the years that followed, there was no question now as to whose word was law in Rome.

---

31 B.C.E.) saw the Egyptian navy destroyed, although thousands of soldiers and sailors are believed to have died on both sides. Antony and Cleopatra took what ships they had left and fled back to Egypt.

As badly as it had gone for Antony, this should have been no more than an opening skirmish. After all, he had a large army on shore in Egypt. When the news came in from Actium, however, his troops started deserting. He is said to have lost 19 legions of infantry and 12,000 mounted cavalry overnight. Even so, he managed to see off the first army Octavian sent against him. But the writing was on the wall, and Antony's men continued to give up on what they saw as a lost cause.

Soon that is what it was. In August 30 B.C.E., Antony found his army heavily outnumbered and surrounded. He was close to despair in any case when

Stern, severe and utterly imperial, a model of political rectitude: Augustus would have liked his portrayal by the seventeenth-century painter Peter Paul Rubens. Octavian (as he was originally known) invented the office of Emperor, but set a standard of which most of his successors would fall short.

the news reached him that Cleopatra had committed suicide. He stabbed himself with his sword, but stayed alive long enough to die in Cleopatra's arms. In reality, Egypt's queen was still alive, but effectively a captive with Octavian now the master in Alexandria. On witnessing her lover's death, however, Cleopatra had no desire to prolong her life. She had two asps (highly poisonous snakes) smuggled to her in a basket of figs. The ancient sources disagree: some say she left the snakes in the basket as she picked at the figs so that death would come unexpectedly by a type of lottery; others say that she took an asp and held it up to her breast, assuming control of her destiny.

Caesarion, Julius Caesar's son, was by now a young man of 17, quite old enough to succeed his mother on Egypt's throne. But Octavian, stating simply that 'Two Caesars are one too many,' had him murdered as a potential rival. The way was now clear for Octavian to inherit his adoptive father's dictatorship and to dominate the Roman Empire, as Caesar had never quite had the chance to do.

EMPEROR AT LAST

Octavian arrived back in Rome to find its senators in doubt. While they praised the returning hero publicly, they were wary of giving him more power. Caesar's rise had given them pause. On the other hand, it was a great relief to have a resolution to the lengthy rivalry between Octavian and Antony, and to have just one dominant figure to deal with in the Empire. In 27 B.C.E. they gave him the honorific name Augustus ('splendid'), and also the title Princeps, which meant the 'first'. No one had formally proclaimed him Emperor, as such. Although he was seems to have grown into an emperor by slow degrees in the years that followed, there was no question now as to whose word was law in Rome.

Even now, Augustus made a point of being unassuming. He discouraged flatterers who suggested that he was some sort of king. He was protesting far too much, though. He, and he alone, was now the unchallenged authority in the Empire; the Roman Republic was no more.

THE FIRST CAESARS

In 27 B.C.E., Octavian took the name Augustus ('splendid') and the title Imperator. Single-handedly, he had created the office of Emperor. But barely had he done so than it was being brought into disrepute – first by his daughter, then by his successor.

The official record shows Augustus' reign as one of prosperity and success, and that is true enough, as far as it goes. It helped that the first Emperor held sway for so long. For 41 years in all, his authority was unquestioned. So, too, for that matter, was Rome's. The *Pax Romana* ('Roman Peace') now established in the Empire was to continue from Augustus' reign for nearly another 200 years. After so many decades of civil strife, a return to order came as a huge relief for the people living under Roman authority. That Augustus, in

The Empire's first official head of state, Augustus made himself the face of Rome: his profile was displayed upon the Empire's coinage (above). Although the statues no doubt exaggerated his authoritative air, all agreed that he cut a commanding figure.

his days as Octavian, had himself caused so much of the trouble was mostly forgotten. What mattered was that he was now presiding over peace.

And he had made Rome great. Who could doubt that when, year by year, they saw yet more grandiose public buildings going up around the capital? 'I found a city of brick,' Augustus was to say, 'and left it one of marble.' That may have been an exaggeration, but he did have a point. Contrast that public grandeur with the simplicity of Augustus' private life. Augustus was ostentatiously unassuming, and he had a busy propaganda machine making sure that everyone knew just how modestly he lived.

His beloved wife, Livia Drusilla, became the iconic Roman wife: devoted, loyal, tough and a little bit severe. Livia Augusta, as she was known after her husband's promotion to the rank of Emperor, made sure that she presented herself as her husband's helpmeet. She was beautiful, but worked hard not to flaunt it. Her straight, simple gown announced a no-frills personality. Her hair was neat, but styled in a way that showed her discipline and restraint. She let it to be known that she spent her time weaving and performing other womanly – but never frivolously 'feminine' – tasks. Livia Augusta had no greater ambition than to uphold the dignity of Rome.

She stood by her man with most admirable selflessness, even to the point, it is said, of bringing

The title 'Imperator' was a military one, meaning 'man who gives the orders', or 'general'. The Emperor's primary role was as commander-in-chief. Years of civil war had equipped Augustus well; here he makes his victorious entry into Syria, around 27 B.C.E.

him virgins to deflower. Dignity was what mattered. As long as adultery didn't jeopardize the reputation of the house it didn't count as adultery at all. Slave girls did not count either, so there was really no reason for Livia to worry about what her husband got up to, as long as her prestige as 'Livia Augusta' remained secure.

HAIR WARS

Livia Augusta was closely associated with the hairstyle known as the *nodus,* or 'knot', which was the height of fashion in the early Roman Empire. It took its name from the topknot that was worn aligned with the centre of the forehead. While waves of hair swept back over the ears hinted at a more obviously feminine softness, these were tied up behind in a crisp, no-nonsense bun. The overall effect was elegant but austere. Like so much in Livia's and Augustus' lives, there was a clear concern that, having seized such absolute power, the imperial couple should be seen as simple servants of the state, upholding the traditional values of the Republic.

But the *nodus* made another statement, too, which becomes clearer when you realize that, though it might have been Livia who made the style really fashionable, it was her sister-in-law Octavia who had actually launched it. Augustus' sister had, of course, been married to Mark Antony in 40 B.C.E. to establish friendly relations between Octavian and his rival. But Antony hadn't waited for his seven-year itch; just three years later he had left Octavia and Rome and returned to Egypt, where he took up with Cleopatra once again.

This was an infidelity not just to Octavia, but, to Octavian and to Rome, a point that Octavian's supporters worked hard to drive home. By adopting the *nodus,* Octavia wasn't giving herself a makeover: she was making her stand as the embodiment of Roman womanhood. Her hair, in its severity, contrasted starkly with the interloper Cleopatra's elaborate coiffure. Octavia was making it clear that she was no Egyptian temptress, no oriental *femme fatale.*

The high-born Roman woman, like this matron of the first century C.E., was a walking advertisement for Roman values. As popularized by Livia Augusta, the *nodus,* or 'knot', displayed the feminine face to full advantage, although the hairstyle is definitely severe by our standards.

Augustus ordered spectacular building projects, not only in Rome but across the Empire as well. This awe-inspiring outdoor theatre in Orange, France, and the regular public shows that were presented here, underlined the power and prestige – and the generosity – of the Emperor who endowed them.

Livia's admirable matter-of-factness was underlined when, one day, walking through the palace, she came across a group of men who were naked after some exercise. By rights they should have been summarily executed, having compromised the purity of the Empress's presence, but Livia gave the order that they should be spared. The sight of a naked man, she said, was no more disconcerting for a woman who was truly chaste than the sight of a marble statue would be.

FAMILY VALUES
Augustus saw no inconsistency (no Roman would have done) between his little liaisons with concubines and his aggressive public campaign for 'family values'. He executed one freedman whom he had long regarded as a personal friend because of his

adulterous relationships with aristocratic wives. It was the offence to Rome's noble households, and therefore to the social status quo, that Augustus objected to in such relationships. He was unconcerned about any moral issues or the emotional hurt that such adultery might cause.

He felt so strongly about the potential upheaval to society that adultery could cause that Augusts brought in legislation outlawing it: a husband who caught his

> Augustus saw no inconsistency between his little liaisons with concubines and his aggressive public campaign for 'family values'.

wife with a lover was legally entitled to kill them both. The same right existed for a father who caught his daughter in adultery. A husband who learned of his wife's infidelity had not just a right but a duty to divorce her within 60 days; she would be banished, and face financial penalties. Women were forbidden to appear in a wide range of public places, and there was a duty in both sexes to marry. Men under 60 and women under 50 were obliged to wed if they were single: if they failed to do so they lost the right to inherit property.

AN UNDUTIFUL DAUGHTER

The imperial couple may have presented a powerfully united front to Rome and the world, but behind the scenes all was not quite as calm as it appeared. Livia was the Emperor's third wife. While he had returned

his first bride, Clodia, to her father 'untouched', already seeing more dynastically advantageous possibilities in a marriage to Scribonia, the daughter of an ally, that second marriage had been a disappointment, to put it mildly. By all accounts, Octavian had been worn out by Scribonia's nagging: her one redeeming act, he claimed, was to have borne

Seated in his rightful place among the gods – and attracting respectful glances, even in this company – Augustus can leave the work of conquest to his victorious soldiers, shown below. After his death, Augustus was quite genuinely worshipped as a deity, as was his Empress, Livia Augusta.

Idlers drink and gossip outside Agrippa's house in this painting by Sir Lawrence Alma-Tadema. One leans back casually against the plinth on which the Emperor's statue stands with its right arm raised in an ironic gesture of command. Augustus' authority was as badly undermined by his daughter's dissolute lifestyle as his friend Agrippa's was from being her husband.

him a baby daughter. That done, he divorced Scribonia on the very same day: she rose from her bed having given birth to find herself a single woman.

Octavian's gratitude for his daughter Julia did not survive long past her infancy. Brought up by himself and Livia, she was a rebel. Her first marriage, to her cousin Marcellus, might have worked out if he had not been taken ill and died on a military campaign in Spain. Her second, to Agrippa, an ally of Augustus, 25 years her senior, was disastrous. It did yield two grandsons for the Emperor, Gaius Caesar and Lucius

Caesar, whom a delighted Augustus adopted and groomed as his successors. Julia didn't get anything she wanted out of the marriage, however, and soon began a long-term love affair with one Sempronius Gracchus. And he, the gossips maintained, was the first of many.

In 12 B.C.E., Agrippa died. Augustus promptly arranged another marriage for his daughter, this time to his stepson Tiberius. He had been born to Livia in a previous marriage but, like Gaius and Lucius Caesar, was taken up by the Emperor as his own. This marriage, too, was a mismatch from the start, but

'I found a city of brick, and left it one of marble.' Augustus' boast was no idle one; his redevelopment of the Forum was especially impressive. The Emperor made a point of the contrast between his ostentatiously simple private life and the splendour of his public building schemes.

Every time he saw Agrippina, Tiberius recalled his humiliation at her mother's hands; their relationship only worsened as time went by. Rubens presents them here in profile – they were never to see eye to eye.

His bust exudes authority, but increasingly Augustus was being exposed to ridicule as a result of his daughter's drunken escapades and illicit sexual liaisons. In the end, the Emperor had to show that he was master in his own house by making a public example of Julia and her lovers.

Julia's sins were now doubly damaging because she was not only bringing disrepute upon the ruling family with her outrageous adulteries, but was also doing so at the expense of a husband who was himself a member of that family. And she was doing it openly. Rome was abuzz with gossip about all her affairs and her very public nightly drinking parties in the Forum. This was at a time when her father had introduced laws demanding that women should barely be seen in public, even in the daytime. That a woman should be out drinking with men at night was beyond the pale. In the circumstances, it is difficult to avoid the suspicion that Julia was driven by a determination to humiliate her father, the Emperor, as deeply as she could.

Augustus certainly had no alternative but to act. By rights, he should have had his daughter executed. He did have the most open and unabashed of her lovers, Iullus Antonius, forced into committing suicide. Sempronius Gracchus got away with exile, as did several other men. Julia, too

A MOTHER'S LOVE?

Inevitably, perhaps, it was whispered in Rome that Livia Augusta had been behind the deaths of both Gaius and Lucius Caesar, anxious to ensure the succession of her son at the expense of Julia's. Certainly, their untimely passing did Tiberius' claims no harm: he moved from third in line to heir apparent in just two years. Some went further, suggesting that, having cleared her son's way this far, Livia then proceeded to remove the final obstacle. The devoted wife, this version of the story goes, attending her husband at dinner, with her own fair hand proffered the figs that poisoned him.

Livia was certainly a tough and determined woman, and an assured political operator. However, there is nothing in the way of evidence, nor even any agreement among the ancient writers, to support this view of Livia as murderess. It is hard to see how the Empress could possibly have been responsible for Gaius Caesar's death of wounds sustained in battle in the Caucasus, and there is no evidence to suggest anything sinister about the illnesses that carried off Lucius Caesar and Augustus.

In the unlikely event that Livia did contrive these deaths to place Tiberius on the throne, it was surely the gravest of miscalculations on her part. Everything we know about his reign tells us that he was dragged along unwillingly and that he was never really reconciled to his position. And if she was hoping for his gratitude, she had misjudged her son still further. From the first he resented what he saw as his mother's meddling. Things only worsened as time went on, and within a few years the breach between them was complete. When she died in 29 C.E., he refused to allow her to be deified alongside her late husband Augustus and had her retrospectively stripped of all her titles.

Germanicus earned his triumphant reception in Rome through his conquests in Germania and the east, but the greater the adulation of Germanicus, the more bitter the Emperor's envy. Once a great general himself, Tiberius felt out of his depth as ruler; his helplessness brought out a spiteful, vicious side.

was exiled, sent to the offshore island of Pandateria (Ventotene) with Scribonia, her mother. She was allowed no contact with men, and no luxuries, even wine. Augustus, deeply embittered, would never refer to her thereafter except as his 'cancer'. Underneath his anger appears to have been very real hurt.

A SAD SUCCESSION

Tiberius had made a most reluctant husband for Julia, not least because he had been happily married at the time when she was widowed. He appears to have genuinely loved his wife Vipsania Agrippina. They had a son, and she was expecting their second child. But the Roman male, especially when he was a member of the imperial household, was not expected to let

sentiment stand in the way of a smart dynastic match. Marriage with Julia would help to keep the succession that much more securely 'in the family'.

And so Vipsania had to make way. The order came from Augustus that Tiberius had to divorce his wife

and wed his stepsister instead. In shock, Vipsania miscarried. Tiberius did his duty and married Julia, but he appears to have been heartbroken by the loss of his beloved wife. One day when Tiberius saw Vipsania out in public, he followed her pathetically in tears.

It was contrived to look like a natural death, but few were in any doubt: Germanicus had been poisoned on the Emperor's orders. Far from securing Tiberius' position, the murder only made him feel more vulnerable: he was practically driven mad by his fear of assassination.

From the first, Tiberius loathed Julia just as passionately as he had loved Vipsania. And Julia, of course, did her best to justify his disgust. While she drank, caroused and slept around, he threw himself into his public duties, serving with distinction with the army in Hungary and Germany. (Military historians see him as one of Rome's greatest generals.) He pursued his political career as well, making a mark for himself in public life. Notwithstanding these

> A decade later, Augustus himself fell ill: 'How did you like the performance?' were his dying words.

achievements, he seems to have lost his sense of direction, and the writer Pliny the Elder described him as *tristissimus hominum* (the 'saddest of men').

Abruptly, and without explanation, in 6 B.C.E. Tiberius retired from public life and went to live in isolation on the island of Rhodes. Augustus was enraged, seeing this as tantamount to deserting his post. A few months after leaving, Tiberius regretted his decision and sought permission to return to Rome. But Augustus, still infuriated, flatly refused, telling Tiberius that he should stay right where he was. Not until 2 C.E. was he finally allowed to come back to the capital, and then only as an ordinary citizen. By now, though, the field of Augustus' heirs was quickly thinning. That same year, Gaius Caesar had died in Armenia; Lucius fell ill and died just two years later. Augustus now formally adopted Tiberius as his son.

A decade later, Augustus himself fell ill: 'How did you like the performance?'

The bust captures her beauty, but offers no hint of the ferocity with which Agrippina would fight for the interests of herself and of her sons. Along with her mother's wayward courage, she had a fanatical family loyalty Julia had lacked: a formidable combination, as the Emperor found.

were his dying words. Having created the role of Emperor himself, he had played the part to perfection. Few of his successors were to rule with such unchallenged authority. Tiberius was particularly badly equipped to occupy Augustus's position, but for better or worse, he was to reign as his successor.

AN ENVIOUS EMPEROR

Tiberius had no relish for the job, and he allowed the state to drift. The Senate, the real power in Republican Rome, had grown weak under successive dictatorships, but Tiberius tried to get it to take back the reins of government. If he was uncomfortable in power himself, though, he did not want anybody else to have any, and he had resented what he saw as Livia's interference. In fact, what made her advice more galling was the fact that he so obviously needed it, and her competence only underlined his own shortcomings.

In the same way, he felt threatened by the military successes of Germanicus. Augustus, before he died, had ordered Tiberius to take this grandson of Livia as his adopted son. Germanicus Julius Caesar Claudianus, to give him his full name, had inherited his honorific *agnomen* from his father, who won major conquests in Germany. But Germanicus the younger might just as well have won it in his own right, given the swathe he was now cutting through a Germania which had in recent years seen a number of rebellions.

That Tiberius should have envied Germanicus is particularly sad because he had been such an accomplished general himself. By now, however, his military exploits lay some way in the past, and he was plainly feeling disorientated and out of his depth. On the news of Tiberius' accession, there had been unrest in the army across the Empire: Germanicus had been the choice both of the generals and the lower ranks. The young man himself had quelled the disturbances, declaring himself fully behind Tiberius, even though he himself was very much the man of the moment.

As Prefect of Tiberius' Praetorian Guard, Sejanus was Rome's most powerful official, with a role in every aspect of the administration of the Empire. Between his uncontainable ambition and the lackadaisical indifference of the Emperor, Sejanus was able to make himself the real power in Rome.

Suddenly, in 18 C.E., while he was on campaign in Asia, Germanicus fell ill. His decline was rapid, and he very quickly died. It had all been extremely sudden – too sudden, many felt, to have been natural. Stories were spreading that he had been poisoned on the Emperor's orders. His widow, Agrippina, came back to Rome with his ashes in an urn, and their six children. They made a desperately disconsolate tableau as they stood at Augustus' tomb where they had trooped together to lay Germanicus' remains to rest. Crowds came out to see them and wept to see their plight, but grief very swiftly turned to anger. Bills reading 'Give us back Germanicus!' were posted up around the city,

and anonymous voices rang out in the night, denouncing those who had killed the people's preferred choice for Emperor.

FINGER OF SUSPICION

Many pointed the finger at the Emperor's friend, the former Governor of Syria Gnaeus Calpurnius Piso. It had been in his sometime province, in Antioch, that Germanicus had died. The two were known to have argued on a number of occasions. Germanicus had ejected Piso from his position, so Piso had his own motive for murder. On the other hand, there was the possibility that Piso had been acting on Tiberius' orders, and there was certainly no shortage of people prepared to believe that theory.

Any idea the Emperor might have had of turning a blind eye to Germanicus' murder (if murder it had been) was ruled out when Piso seized the opportunity to take back Syria for himself. Was this a reward from

PERVERSE PLEASURES

In Capri, Tiberius gave himself over entirely to debauchery. He built a special villa in which he could realize his wildest fantasies. Its walls were decorated throughout with pornographic paintings, and there was a library of erotic books so that the Emperor and his guests would never be at a loss for inspiration. To entertain and arouse them, groups of catamites performed together three at a time. Outside in the grounds were secluded grottoes where boys and girls dressed as deities or nymphs waited to entice the wanderer inside.

It was even said that he had little boys trained to swim in and out between his legs as he bathed, licking and biting his body as they went by. Toddlers were left unweaned, simply so that they would suck instinctively at his penis, as if it were a teat.

Capri was a world away from Rome, from the cares of command, the responsibilities of office: here Tiberius could indulge his fantasies of endless idleness and pleasure. Back in the Empire's capital, however, Sejanus was clawing his way to power. Ultimately, he planned to overthrow the Emperor's rule.

the Emperor for faithful service? Everything looked damning, as far as the public were concerned, and Tiberius' hand was forced. He felt that he had no alternative but to hold a trial. Piso committed suicide (or so it appeared), before he could face his accusers. Was this an admission of guilt on the governor's part?

Or was it, more sinister still, that the Emperor had ordered Piso's murder to cover up his involvement in Germanicus' death?

Germanicus' widow, Agrippina, was the daughter of the faithless Julia by Agrippa, her second husband, and not surprisingly there was no love lost between her and

Tiberius. Julia had died within a few months of the father with whom she had never really been reconciled. The new Emperor, her estranged husband, had held her under house arrest. She had died of malnutrition, which was highly unusual for a woman of her rank. There were claims that Tiberius had ordered her guards to stop feeding her altogether in her confinement, until, after a long, agonizing decline, she starved to death.

Although she was a truer wife than her mother had been, Agrippina had much the same headstrong courage. She accused her father-in-law to his face of soliciting her husband's murder. Furious, the Emperor had her banished from his company for some years. Tiberius and his mother, Livia, were

> There were claims that Tiberius had ordered Julia's guards to stop feeding her altogether in her confinement, until, after a long, agonizing decline, she starved to death.

united in their suspicion of Agrippina's motives. It was an open secret that Agrippina believed that Germanicus' sons – Nero Caesar, Drusus Caesar and Gaius Julius Caesar ('Caligula') – should be in the forefront of the imperial succession.

A MURDEROUS PLOT

Tiberius' paranoia was selective: alert as he had been to the threat from Germanicus, he remained completely oblivious to the danger that he faced from another source. He implicitly trusted his friend and adviser Lucius Aelius Sejanus, whom he had made Prefect of the Praetorian Guard. Originally this had been the Emperor's personal bodyguard. They were an elite unit, and had no political significance. But Sejanus had slowly and surely been building it up to be an important arm of the state and a formidable personal military power base. Tiberius had been only too happy to let him get on with it, pleased to find someone else taking up his responsibilities of state.

Ruthless, cunning and ferociously ambitious, Sejanus was resolved to make it to the very top, but there was a very obvious obstacle to that ascent. This was Julius Caesar Drusus, Tiberius' son by his first wife Vipsania, and the heir he had appointed to succeed him to the throne. The two had long been wary of each other.

Soon Sejanus was plotting to get rid of his rival, once and for all. He set about getting as close as he possibly could to Drusus' wife, Livilla. She was a granddaughter of Livia, after whom she had been named. She had all her grandmother's ambition, which she may well have felt was liable to be thwarted once Augustus had made Tiberius adopt Germanicus as his son. Although Drusus was the Emperor's son, and had performed creditably both in Roman politics and in the field of war, he had clearly been overshadowed by Germanicus' glittering career. Far from removing this threat, Germanicus' death had propelled his widow, Agrippina, into the limelight, allowing her to lobby relentlessly for her three sons.

Sejanus wooed Livilla, and soon they were secret lovers. He does not appear to have encountered much resistance, and, although Sejanus was a compelling personality, it seems most likely that Livilla was primarily seduced by her ambition. Drusus, she had decided, was a bad bet. Her best hope of becoming Empress would be as fellow conspirator with the Prefect. She was not one to lose her head. Conscious that Sejanus might only too possibly be planning to double-cross her, she made him divorce his wife Apicata and leave his three children, to show he meant marital business. Once this had been done, in 23 C.E., the happy couple acted together to kill Livilla's husband. Her personal physician Eudemus administered the poison. So subtle was it in its action that Drusus appeared to be suffering from some natural illness; he died slowly over the course of several days.

EXILE AGAIN

The death of Drusus disturbed Tiberius – although less, perhaps, on account of his bereavement than as a result of the heightened sense of vulnerability it left him with, even though as yet there was no suggestion foul play. Far from making him more determined to assert his authority, it only served to distract him from the business of government, making him even more reliant on his Prefect.

His paranoia was growing. When Agrippina sought his permission to remarry in 26 C.E., Tiberius began to

A ROMAN MOTHER

Antonia Minor was the daughter of Augustus' sister, Octavia, by Mark Antony, athough he had of course left his Roman family for Cleopatra. That betrayal, of both home and country, had only steeled his daughter's Roman resolve. She was the niece the Emperor preferred above all others, and her aunt Livia also seems to have taken an interest in her from a very early age. In fact, Antonia was to name her only daughter after Livia.

Very much a daughter of the establishment, Antonia grew up to marry the general and consul Nero Claudius Drusus. One of her sons was himself a general, the celebrated Germanicus; the other, the future Emperor Claudius. When her husband was killed in action, the Emperor urged her to remarry, but Antonia refused, preferring to stand by the memory of her late husband.

A formidable woman, then, and although not without a love for power and its trappings for herself and her family, her ultimate loyalty lay with Rome itself.

Women in Rome were very much the second sex, but that did not mean that they could not command respect: the loyal matron was regarded with reverent awe. Antonia Minor was exemplary: thanks to her steadfastness and her courage, Sejanus' rise was stopped, and the Empire saved.

brood upon her motives and her dynastic aspirations. He was encouraged in his anxieties by Sejanus, who himself saw Agrippina's sons as a serious threat. Agrippina's ambitions on their behalf were no secret, although the Emperor's reaction still seems disproportionate: he had her banished to Pandateria, where her mother had been sent before her.

But Tiberius, too, was heading off into exile. It may well have been his fear of assassination that lay behind his decision effectively to retire for a second time. That same year, he took himself off to the island of Capri. He left Rome to the tender mercies of Sejanus, now firmly established as Livilla's lover. Only the aged Livia stood between the Prefect and his ambitions.

SEJANUS MAKES HIS MOVE

By the end of the decade, Sejanus' influence was at its height. In Tiberius' absence, he was effectively running Rome. Over the years, he had built up the Praetorian Guard from a small corps to a substantial force some 12,000 strong, to all intents and purposes his own private army. He had the Emperor where he wanted him: dependent on him for information on what was happening in the Empire and the imperial capital. He was potentially the ruler of the Roman world, but not yet in reality.

However important Sejanus had grown, he was still a functionary, and he had his eye on the prize of absolute power. If Livia's death in 29 C.E. came as a

Sejanus came within an ace of seizing the imperial throne for himself, before his conspiracy was exposed by Antonia Minor. Uproar erupted on the streets of Rome as the Emperor Tiberius took charge and the people turned on the Prefect and his supporters.

relief to Tiberius, it was even more welcome to Sejanus, who now felt emboldened enough to launch his assault on the imperial throne. He began by embarking on a series of treason trials, aimed at the most important families in the Roman establishment. The proceedings were a cynical sham, with the prosecutions based on the spurious 'evidence' of his paid informers; the intention was to neutralize any opposition to Sejanus' rise. Rome was gripped by fear and suspicion, and many honest patrician citizens committed suicide, rather than fall victim to Sejanus' men.

AGRIPPINA'S END

Naturally, Sejanus singled out Agrippina and her family for special attention. Tiberius needed no persuading that Drusus' widow was a potent threat. Already banished to Pandateria, she was now arrested along with Nero and Drusus Caesar, her two eldest sons. The former, tried for treason, was either murdered or committed suicide. Drusus, too, was convicted, and starved to death in prison. Agrippina was herself incarcerated, and treated with the most appalling brutality. After one beating she even lost an eye. When she tried to take her life by starving herself to death, she was violently force-fed: she would not escape the cruelty of the Emperor and his Prefect so easily. Not until four years later would Agrippina be allowed to waste away, leaving behind her three daughters and her youngest son, Gaius Julius Caesar, or 'Caligula'.

A boyish 17, Caligula seems to have disarmed Tiberius with his apparent ingenuousness. Indeed, he became something of a pet. In 31 C.E., the Emperor took Caligula to live with him in Capri. While it was hardly the most appropriate environment for an adolescent boy, given all the goings-on, it did have the advantage of keeping him alive.

BEFORE A FALL

In 25 C.E., Sejanus had sought the Emperor's permission to marry Livilla. Tiberius had refused the request, and in no uncertain terms. Although remarkably tolerant of Sejanus' politicking, he had clearly seen this as a move too far. Seeing his friend's

According to a much later legend, amid moves to make him a god, Augustus consulted the old wise-woman, the Sibyl. She showed the awestruck Emperor a vision of the Virgin Mary with the infant Christ, proclaiming 'This child will be greater than thou.' This painting by the Renaissance artist Paris Bordone depicts Augustus visiting the Sibyl amid imagined Roman architecture.

reaction, Sejanus had hastily backtracked. Six years on, however, he felt much bolder. In 31 C.E., Sejanus announced his betrothal to Livilla.

It was, we are told, Sejanus' prospective mother-in-law who finally called him to account. Antonia Minor was one of the most formidable women of her time. Secretly, she sent a letter to the Emperor in Capri, warning him of her daughter and the Prefect's plans. They were, she said, conspiring to murder both Tiberius himself and Caligula, so that Sejanus might be installed on the imperial throne.

At last, Tiberius woke up to the threat his old friend and adviser had always posed. He was as decisive now as he had been lackadaisical before. Rushing straight to Rome, he asserted his authority, and those who had been browbeaten into backing Sejanus now either rallied to the Emperor or at least withdrew to see what would happen. Either way, the firm power base Sejanus had built suddenly started to look shaky. Tiberius followed through by conferring priesthood on Caligula, an implicit seal of his sponsorship. As Sejanus' support

continued to ebb, the Emperor appointed Naevius Sutorius Macro to replace him as Prefect. Sejanus was summoned to appear before the Senate.

The scene was dramatic. Tiberius still felt called upon to proceed with the utmost caution, so Sejanus had been told he was about to be offered a prestigious new position. His letter, read before the assembly, started off with fulsome praise, basically buying time while Macro took command of the Praetorian Guard and had the Senate House surrounded. Only some way into the script did the true import of the Emperor's letter emerge. Abruptly, it changed tack, attacking Sejanus and demanding his arrest.

A HEADLONG DESCENT

That night, a second Senate meeting decreed that Sejanus should be put to death. He was strangled and his body hurled down the Gemonian Steps in the heart of Rome. For three days, it was left at the mercy of the mob, which tore it limb from limb, and left the remains for dogs and crows to pick at. A festival of bloodletting now broke out as angry bands roamed the city, settling scores. Those who had risen with Sejanus now fell with him and had to pay. They were dragged from their homes and killed. Meanwhile, with the order going out for a *damnatio memoriae* ('damnation of the memory') to be placed on Sejanus, statues and inscriptions commemorating him were destroyed, and he was officially erased from the public record.

Sejanus' son was executed. His mother, Alpicata, committed suicide, but not before sending a letter to the Emperor telling him that there had been more to Drusus' death eight years before than had met the eye. Livilla's slaves confessed under torture that they had given poison to the Emperor's son on the instructions of their mistress. Tiberius handed Livilla over to her mother, but she was to find no pity there. Antonia confined her to a room, the story goes, and let her starve. A *damnatio memoriae* was placed upon her, too.

A DISMAL END

Tiberius seems never to have recovered. He had been doubly shocked, not just by Sejanus' treason, but also by his discovery that Drusus had been murdered. He may, as Tacitus and Suetonius claimed, have been unmoved by Drusus' death, but he was certainly shaken by the thought that he had been murdered. Once again, his fears for his safety, far from prompting

him to seize control of the situation, caused him to relinquish the reins of government and let things drift.

He was energetic only in his pursuit of treachery. Executions were held daily, without regard for festivals or holy days. Entire families – men, women and children – were arraigned together and, as no one was ever acquitted, they invariably went to their deaths together, too. Between bribery and terror, the justice system was completely corrupted. Children turned informers against their parents. Many attempted to cheat the executioner by taking poison or slashing their wrists. But if they were found in time, they would be dragged out to be publicly put to death.

The Roman 'justice' system had become a killing machine. Those convicted were grabbed with a sharp iron hook and dragged to the top of the Gemonian Steps to be strangled before being hurled down, still gasping and twitching, to be finished off by the crowd, then simply left to rot. One day saw no fewer than 20

> Sejanus was strangled and his body hurled down the Gemonian Steps in the heart of Rome. For three days it was left at the mercy of the mob, which tore it limb from limb and left the remains for dogs and crows to pick at. A festival of bloodletting now broke out.

of these state-sponsored lynchings. By law it was forbidden for virgins to be strangled. Scrupulously, then, the executioner would rape any maiden who fell into his hands, before continuing with his work in the usual way.

In the end, Tiberius' *imperium* was to limp on for another six years. He died in 37 C.E., aged 77. Legend has it that his paranoid fears were finally realized when he was smothered by Sejanus' successor Nevius Sutorius Macro, perhaps with the assistance of his imperial heir, Caligula. However Tiberious came to die, the news of his passing sparked scenes of jubilation on the streets of Rome: 'Into the Tiber with Tiberius!' was the cry.

II

'LITTLE BOOTS'

There have been all too many monstrous tyrants over the centuries. But even in this outrageous company, Caligula has a special place. His cruelty and capriciousness were breathtaking. His perversity was insane. No crime, it seemed, would ever be beyond him.

◆

Caligula. The name has come to be synonymous with monstrosity, with depravity and cruelty of the basest kind. It is hard to imagine that, when it was first used, it was as an affectionate nickname. The man who succeeded Tiberius as Emperor was Gaius Julius Caesar; the name 'Caligula' had been given him in childhood. Then, as a tiny toddler on campaign with his father Germanicus, he had been paraded before the troops in his own uniform. He made an adorable sight, this little

The sculpted face is no more than a mask: there is resolve, even ruthlessness, in the frown, but no hint here of the scale of Caligula's demented malice. Gaius Julius Caesar took the institution of imperial rule to depths of depravity of which his predecessor Tiberius never dreamt.

legionary, from his helmeted head down to his feet that were neatly shod with miniature versions of the *caligae* (or sandal-boots) the soldiers wore. Far from home, and from their own sons and daughters, the men doted on their general's son, who became a sort of mascot for the army.

In childhood, then, Caligula was a popular pet, and, while he understandably wearied of that role, it was to stand him in good stead as he grew older. Consciously or not, he had learned to play up to it, to work his charm and win people over, and to put people at their ease and assuage their anger. That disarming manner saved his life because, while his elder brothers both fell victims to Tiberius' paranoia, Caligula was taken into the Emperor's household, where he grew up. The idea, to begin with at least, was that he was in Capri as a prisoner, but by slow degrees he turned the situation round. Soon he was the Emperor's pet.

THE PERFORMANCE OF A LIFETIME

Even then, there was a great deal more to Caligula than an engaging smile because his very mildness took an extraordinary effort of will. All around him, people were trying to catch him out, to trap him into indiscreet remarks about Tiberius or complaints about the treatment he and his family had received. Nothing. Caligula couldn't have been happier. It

While Rome was certainly notorious for its orgies, under Tiberius' 'care' in Capri, Caligula grew up surrounded by every sort of vice, perversion and excess (below). As Emperor (opposite), he was to show himself a despot as warped in his desires as he was implacable in his cruelty.

seemed that he couldn't speak too highly of the Emperor or his household. Those who spoke to him saw nothing in his eyes to suggest that he was even conscious of his family's recent history, painfully as it must have been seared into his mind. If Augustus had died with a sense that he had been playing a part in his reign as Emperor, Caligula seems to have been acting all his life.

It was a consummate performance. Beneath the surface, though, something was evidently very badly amiss. Caligula was already displaying disturbing signs. A moralist might have wondered whether a place in which a permanent orgy appeared to be in progress was the ideal home for an impressionable teenage boy. There were no complaints from Caligula, though, and not just because it was his unswerving policy to placate Tiberius – something in the lifestyle suited him.

C · GALIGVLA · CÆS · AVG · IIII · RO · IMP · 4

Ant.° tempe.it fecerunt 1596

Driven, even tormented, by exotic desires, he needed non-stop stimulation. Excess was always insufficient. He binged on food and drink – and on sexual pleasure. There were signs already of a taste for sadism. He liked to watch the Emperor's enemies being tortured, and even Tiberius was taken aback by Caligula's savagery.

IRRESISTIBLE CHARM

Tiberius himself was given to comment that he was bringing up a 'viper' who would one day bite him and would go on to bring about the ruin of Rome itself. And yet Caligula's charm was irresistible. Tiberius not only allowed the boy to live, but also kept him as his constant companion. Tiberius tried to channel his protégé's perversity into an interest in drama, song and dance, and up to a point his strategy seemed to work. But then Caligula's whole life was a theatrical creation already.

Was it he who eventually stage-managed Tiberius' death, making the Emperor's prophecy a reality? There

Song, dance and drama were a regular part of patrician life in Roman times, as this stunning fresco from Pompeii's Hall of Mysteries clearly shows. Tiberius encouraged Caligula's interest in theatrical activities as an outlet for what it was already clear was a serious aggression problem.

were some who suggested that the 'viper' had been behind what was officially put down as a natural end, through sickness. If this was so, it seems certain that he was acting in collaboration with Macro, Tiberius' Prefect, whom Caligula had always been careful to cultivate. Tiberius had been ill for some time, but the suspicion is that the two men may have intervened to hurry his death along and hasten Caligula's succession to the throne. One classical source describes Macro smothering the ailing Emperor with his own pillow.

Named as Imperator on 18 March 37 C.E., Caligula promised a new beginning after the depression, and the increasing tumult, of Tiberius' last years. The people acclaimed the accession of the man they called 'our baby' and 'our star'; the cute little Caligula of childhood had not been forgotten. Nor had his father Germanicus been forgotten, recalled as a victor in the field of battle and a victim, everyone assumed, of an unpopular Emperor's plot.

Tactfully, Caligula played down his relationship with Tiberius, instead emphasizing his connection to Augustus. His mother, Agrippina, had been the first Emperor's granddaughter (even if her mother, Julia, had hardly been the most dutiful of daughters). His father, Germanicus, meanwhile, had been descended from Livia Augusta, through the son of her first

A SON AND A BROTHER

In a spirit of family piety (quite possibly sincere, as far as it went), Caligula made a personal pilgrimage to Pandateria, where his mother had died. He also went to Pontia, the scene of his brother Nero's death. He collected Agrippina's bones, had his brother's scattered ashes gathered together, and brought all these remains back to Rome for a proper burial. No trace could be found of his other brother, Drusus, so Caligula erected a cenotaph to him. Games and festivities were consecrated to the memory of his mother and father.

One of Caligula's first acts as Emperor was to bring home the ashes of his mother and brother, and bury them in their ancestral tomb (right). This underlined Caligula's piety, but also recalled Agrippina's heartrending return from Asia with the relics of his father Germanicus years before (below).

Extraordinary as so many of its achievements were, ancient Rome's was a strikingly savage civilization: people of all classes flocked to see spectacles of fearful cruelty. Men and beasts were baited and slaughtered for entertainment: the more blood the better, apparently, as far as the watching thousands were concerned.

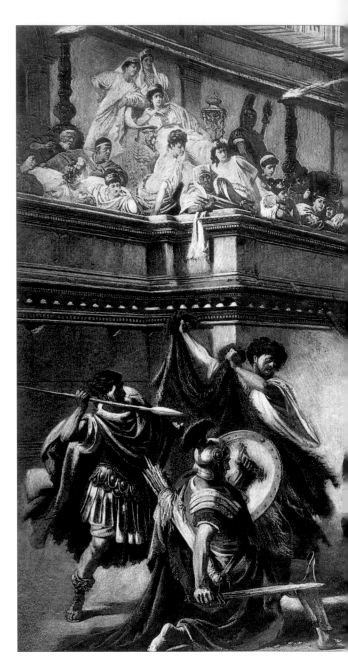

marriage. So concerned was Caligula to establish the link with Augustus that he even suggested that his mother had been born of the incestuous relationship between the first Emperor and his daughter Julia. Caligula took the title of 'Augustus', along with those of *Pontifex Maximus* ('High Priest') and *Pater Patriae* ('Father of the Fatherland').

PUTTING ON A SHOW

To cement his connection with the people, Caligula staged a series of sumptuous shows and games. There were religious ceremonies and sacrifices, horse and chariot races and gladiatorial contests. In the course of these festivities, 160,000 animals were killed. He still had his taste for drama, and sponsored a great many plays. The celebrations continued for three full months, representing not just a welcome diversion for the population, but the beginnings of a cult around the munificent figure of the Emperor as well. Sometimes

> Caligula disappeared from public life for some time. When he came back, he seemed to have undergone a dramatic change.

Caligula didn't bother going through the motions of spreading his largesse through the endowment of such spectacles, but simply had baskets of food, gifts or money handed out to the populace.

The new Emperor's first more formal acts of governance were also more like public bribes than legislative measures. He gave generous bonuses to Rome's soldiers, and relief to those who felt they had been unfairly punished by the imperial excise. Of more genuine significance was the fact that Caligula finally called an end to the treason trials, which had come close to tearing Roman society apart during Tiberius' final years, creating, as they did, a climate of deep fear and suspicion. What amounted to a 'charm offensive'

on the new Emperor's part was masterminded by Macro, who was becoming a power behind the imperial throne.

So where did it all go wrong? About six months into his reign, Caligula was suddenly taken ill; by all accounts, he came very close to death. The frantic activity of his first few months on the throne seems to have brought about some kind of breakdown or

'burnout', although it has also been suggested that the Emperor's long-term problem of epilepsy may have taken a severe turn for the worse. Whatever the cause, Caligula disappeared from public life for some time. When he came back, he seemed to have undergone a dramatic change.

In the first shock of his collapse, there had been extravagant gestures of grief and protestations of devotion to the Emperor. One Roman nobleman, Atanius Secundus, had said publicly that he would happily go into the gladiatorial arena if his *Imperator* were spared; another, Publius Afranius Potitus, had said he would gladly give up his own life if Caligula's were saved. Back from the brink of death, Caligula now decided to hold them to their promises. Secundus was forced to fight for his life as a gladiator.

Fortunately for him, he was to survive. But Potitus was kept to his promise and put to death.

PARANOIA AND PURGE

The killings were by no means over. In the weeks that followed Caligula's recovery, a number of close advisers took their own lives. The Emperor's father-in-law, Marcus Silvanus, was forced to kill himself. (His daughter was already dead: Junia Claudilla had married Caligula in 33 C.E., only to die in childbirth a year later.) Caligula's cousin Tiberius Gemellus was also compelled to commit suicide, as was another counselor, Julius Graecinus. The latter had refused to prosecute his friend Gemellus and so had made himself an accessory to his crime, officially that of plotting against Caligula. There were those who said that the conspiracy had existed only in the Emperor's mind, but that hardly mattered, because Caligula's paranoia was now law.

The biggest beast to be claimed by this cull of potential rivals was the Emperor's closest adviser, Naevius Sutorius Macro. No one had done more than Macro to secure the imperial throne for Caligula, but that apparently counted for nothing now. Or, rather, it counted against him. So formidable a figure was Macro, so influential had he become, that Caligula could all too easily envisage Macro ruling in his place. The Emperor ordered him to Egypt with his wife

Ennia to take up the governorship there, he said, but had them both arrested when they arrived at Ostia, the port of Rome. The couple was taken to prison, where they killed themselves.

FAMILY MAN

It was at about this time that Caligula remarried. He snatched his second wife, Livia Orestilla, at the ceremony where she was in the process of being wed to another man. The story would be romantic if it weren't for its ending,

Agrippina the Younger had her mother's looks, but there the similarity ended: she was as vicious as Agrippina the Elder had been chaste. Wanton, wayward, wily, she was fatally seductive but ruthlessly self-seeking, a woman who would stop at nothing to get her way.

which came just a few days later when the Emperor had second thoughts and divorced her. She was still his property, though, as far as he was concerned. When, some time later, he started to suspect she was seeing her original, intended husband, he was enraged, and reacted by sending her into exile.

Lollia Paulina, whom he married in 37 C.E., lasted a full six months before it became clear that she was infertile and he divorced her.

Not that the Emperor had to forgo the pleasure of female company between these marriages, nor was he confined to the marital couch while they were going on. His three sisters notoriously became his concubines. Of these, the eldest was Agrippina the Younger, who could hardly have been more different than her mother 'Agrippina the Elder'. That thorn in Tiberius' flesh, Germanicus' widow, had been the model of the heroically faithful Roman wife. Her eldest daughter was a beautiful but baneful temptress.

Her younger sisters were hardly any better. Drusilla, who came next in age, was the one her brother preferred. She divorced two husbands on his orders. An unnatural attachment it may have been, but it was also a very strong one. When Drusilla died of a fever in 38 C.E., the Emperor was left desolate, and barely able to carry on. He gave her the title Augusta, reserved for an empress, and had her deified by order of the Senate. He himself insisted on swearing oaths by the name of this *Diva Drusilla* ('Goddess Drusilla') and never recovered from the agony of her loss. The

As the wine flowed, the inhibitions ebbed: the great banquets of the Roman Emperors were a scene for every conceivable kind of debauchery. But even by these standards, Caligula's orgies were extreme: he would publicly couple with his own sisters, it was said.

youngest of his sisters, Julia Livilla, was also said to have been his mistress, but she was never as important to him as Drusilla had been.

PUBLIC PLEASURES

Far from concealing his incestuous passions, Caligula flaunted them. He would dally with his sisters openly at formal banquets. As the evening wore on and the mood relaxed, they would become more overtly sexual, often making love in front of everyone. Sometimes the wife of the time would be told to join in, lying on top of her husband as he embraced one or other of his sisters.

Roman ladies of noble families must have dreaded these big banquets – as, indeed, their husbands must have done. Politically, they could not afford to miss these state events. To offend the Emperor might very easily mean torture and death, and the confiscation of the family's estate on some trumped-up charge. But the banquet itself was a terrible ordeal. Caligula treated it as a cattle market in which he appraised his nobles' wives like so much livestock. He would look them over as they walked past his couch, perhaps detaining them with his hand to check their eyes, teeth or chin, or any other feature that had attracted his curiosity.

> Sometimes he produced a parody, setting the oldest, most useless gladiators against the mangiest, most decrepit animals, or staging fights between the physically disabled.

A little later in the proceedings, he would send a slave over to summon this or that woman, and make an ostentatious show of retiring with her to an adjoining room. Her husband would have to smile gracefully through this rigmarole, and maintain his cheerful aspect afterwards as Caligula went over his wife's physical beauties and blemishes before the entire company and gave his verdict on her sexual performance.

POWER GAMES

The Emperor was undeniably a sadist. He delighted in the discomfiture and pain of others. He found

Caligula dines with Incitatus, the horse he held in higher regard than most of his officials. He even contemplated having him appointed consul. It is hard to know how far behaviour of this kind stemmed from serious insanity and how far from a desire to humiliate his human courtiers.

their fear delicious. At one banquet he suddenly burst out laughing and, when asked the reason, replied that the thought had just struck him that a nod on his part would be enough to see them put to death. But if he found the power of life and death to be exhilarating, it was closely associated for him with his sense of sexual prowess. As he nuzzled the neck of a wife or mistress, he would murmur excitedly that it might be struck through at once if he were only to decide to give the order.

Officials were often subjected to petty humiliations. Some were made to run for miles alongside his chariot in their long, flowing togas, the Emperor enjoying their humiliation, their exhaustion and their fear. Others had to take off their patrician togas and stand around in their short tunics, like slaves, attending on him while he took his meals.

The gratuitousness of his cruelty is striking. He liked to play practical jokes of a sort that would have seemed infantile had they not been so serious for their victims. It is clear that he liked to wrong-foot his public. While he enjoyed his reputation as a generous patron of gladiatorial shows, he occasionally gave the public more than they had bargained for. Sometimes he produced a parody, setting the oldest, most useless gladiators against the mangiest, most decrepit animals, or staging fights between the physically disabled. Sometimes the 'joke' would be on the public itself. He would have the awnings over the terraces taken down in the hottest part of the day and give the order that no one was to be allowed to leave.

SPEND, SPEND, SPEND

It is a common failing to be bad with money, and having the resources of Rome to play with must have been a big temptation. But there was something truly pathological about Caligula's urge to splurge. His profligacy was almost as legendary as his lust and cruelty, and he showed extraordinary ingenuity in coming up with new ways for wasting money. He would dissolve precious pearls in vinegar and drink them; he had his guests' food gold-leafed; he had

jewel-encrusted ships constructed, with baths and porticoes on board. Some of these vessels even boasted gardens with vines and fruit trees so that Caligula and his companions could relax and party under sail, entertained by orchestras and singing groups.

Hills were flattened to clear the way for the vast villa complexes he had built on shore, and he had tunnels constructed through mountainsides of stone. But his engineering mania surely found its most notorious expression when he came up with a way of riding across the Bay of Baiae. Bringing together cargo ships from far and wide, he had them anchored together in two parallel rows extending all the way across the bay a distance of about 5 kilometres (3

miles). He then had earth heaped upon them and graded to create a road-like surface. Once it was finished, he spent the next two days riding back and forth in triumph across this floating highway escorted by his entire Praetorian Guard.

But Caligula did not love money merely for the things that it could buy. He desired it, lusted after it, in a way that was all but sexual. Contemporaries described him making great heaps of gold coinage, frequently in public places. He would walk through it barefoot, or even roll around in it, soaking up the sensation of the chill metal edges against his body.

A HOUSE FOR A HORSE

Monstrous as he was, Caligula could be passionate in his attachments, and Drusilla had been only the most striking example of this tendency. He lavished gifts upon those who took his fancy, of whom none came higher in his estimation than Incitatus, his beloved horse. Caligula treated this trusty steed with a consideration he never seems to have shown to another human. On the eve of an important parade, so as to be sure his horse's slumbers were not disturbed, he would send his soldiers to enforce strict silence in the streets around his stable.

And what a stable it was. Caligula had it completely fitted out in marble, with a manger of ebony. A house was built onto it, luxuriously appointed with rich furnishings and with a full complement of slaves, so that guests might be entertained in style in Incitatus' name. The animal itself had a jewel-encrusted collar and wore blankets richly dyed in imperial purple, as befitted a horse whose master had high hopes of eventually appointing him to the office of consul.

RAISING REVENUE

Such was Caligula's extravagance that, within a year of his accession, he had run through the 2,700,000,000 sesterces with which Tiberius had filled the coffers of the state. (For all his faults, Caligula's predecessor had been very cautious, many said simply stingy, in his spending.) Caligula was always on the lookout for ways of recouping money. One was to turn the imperial palace into a brothel. Not content with sleeping with his sisters, he pimped them out to wealthy guests.

It brought in money, but it was never going to be more than a drop in the ocean of his extravagance. He resorted to desperate measures to raise more funds. He at least had the advantage of being Emperor and a

Jewellery, weapons, slaves, chariots, ships, palaces ... you name it, and Caligula bought it – at the state's expense. Tiberius' careful housekeeping had left the imperial coffers overflowing, but his successor emptied them and then some with his spendthrift ways. Here he buys himself another gladiator.

SAVAGE 'JUSTICE'

Caligula gave orders that executions be performed, not at a stroke, but by a succession of smaller wounds, because he wanted the victim to feel the whole experience of death. Prisoners were tortured or executed to entertain him while he had his lunch. One youth was executed (for foppishness, allegedly) with his father looking on. Caligula then 'cheered up' the old man by making him laugh and joke with him at a banquet. Once, at a public banquet, when one of his slaves was caught stripping silver trimmings from some of the couches, the Emperor had both of his hands cut off. They were then hung around his neck, along with a placard announcing the nature of his crime, and the unfortunate wretch was led around the room among the diners.

Roman justice was always stern and unforgiving, but under Caligula it was worse, subject to his every caprice and cruel whim. Men and women were convicted of all sorts of improbable 'crimes' and put to the most savage punishments, such as having wild animals set upon them, as here.

Right: The statue of Caligula, the god, stands in all its splendour outside his temple – constructed, controversially, by the Emperor himself. Even Augustus had been content to wait for the Roman Senate to ordain his deification, which took place posthumously: Caligula proclaimed himself a god in his own lifetime.

reputation for ruthlessness, which meant that no demand was ever too preposterous to be obeyed. Caligula invented new taxes and tariffs which he arbitrarily imposed on wealthy families. He fabricated criminal cases against rich men and required the payment of massive fines. Many of these so-called trials were really little more than cynical shakedowns. Patrician defendants were held hostage, the ransom to be paid their property.

THE SISTERS STRIKE BACK

In 39 C.E., Caligula discovered that his sisters Agrippina and Julia had been conspiring against him. Was it out of anger, hatred and disgust at what he had done? Perhaps, though it may just as easily have been that, accustomed to the trappings and privileges of power in Rome, they were prepared to stop at nothing to possess even more. By now, both women had become lovers of Drusilla's widower, Marcus

Of all the chapters of Rome's 'dark history', fewer have been darker than the reign of Caligula, a figure of fear for his people – especially his patricians. It was not just his murderous violence but also the complete unpredictability of his moods that made him so utterly terrifying a figure. Here he rages at the moon.

Aemilius Lepidus. They planned to kill Caligula and place Lepidus on the throne.

Unfortunately for them, the conspiracy was discovered and the Emperor had all three put on trial. He himself appeared before the court to bear witness against their characters. He had the effrontery to criticize his sisters for their loose morals. Even so, he spared their lives. Lepidus was executed for his part in the plot, while Agrippina and Julia were sent into exile in the Pontine islands. Their wealth and possessions having been confiscated by Caligula, they were forced to work as sponge-divers to support themselves.

DIVINE MADNESS

It was at around this time that Caligula started demanding to be treated as a god. This was not quite as extraordinary as it may sound. Deceased luminaries were already seen as deities: Julius Caesar, Augustus, even Livia Augusta, all had been deified. In the Asian provinces, it was traditional to see living

> He dressed up variously as Bacchus, god of wine and sexual freedom; Apollo, god of light and healing; and Hercules, the deified superhero. All, of course, represented different models of masculinity that Caligula liked to try out at different times.

rulers as divine, and it seems to have been from here that the custom came to Rome. Caligula was already worshipped in the east of his empire, and there was a special shrine for him at Miletus, in modern Turkey. Despite this, there was absolutely no precedent for a living Emperor to be deified in the west. It was simply sheer megalomania on Caligula's part.

With, perhaps, a touch of something a little more psychosexual, Caligula liked to think that in his divinity he took many different forms. He dressed up variously as Bacchus, god of wine and sexual freedom; Apollo, god of light and healing; and Hercules, the deified superhero. All, of course, represented different models of masculinity that Caligula liked to try out at different times. Not just masculinity, though. He also dressed in drag to represent Juno, queen of the gods and heavenly matriarch; Diana the huntress, and goddess of chastity, and Venus, the goddess of sexual love.

TEMPLE TROUBLE

Caligula's dressing-up games may well have been his way of exploring an ambiguous sexuality, but it would be wrong to assume that his claims to divinity were anything but serious. He had two temples built to himself in Rome. One was on the Capitoline Hill, near Jupiter's temple (he was irritated that the father of the gods had appropriated this prestigious site before him). The other he built on the Palatine. A life-sized statue of Caligula in gold was installed here, and each morning it was dressed exactly as the living Emperor was that day.

A TRICK TRIUMPH

The title the Romans gave their Emperor was *Imperator*, the original meaning of which was just 'general'. The Roman Empire was first and last a military enterprise, and the Emperor's most important function was as commander-in-chief. Augustus had won a major civil war on his way to the imperial throne. With all his shortcomings as Emperor, Tiberius had been a highly successful general. But despite owing much of his early popularity to his status as the son of a famous war hero, Germanicus, Caligula had never really cut it in the field of war.

Worse, the one campaign he had launched, another expedition into Germania in 40 C.E., had come unstuck and had to be withdrawn from in some ignominy. Here, Caligula's theatrical streak asserted itself again. Rather than risk appearing as a failure before his people, he cooked up stories of great exploits among the barbarian tribes. It was easy enough to do this in the absence of modern news media, but what was he going to do about a triumph? It was the tradition for the successful war leader to make a ceremonial procession through the streets of the capital, showing off his prisoners and his captured booty to the cheering crowds. In the absence of either, Caligula was reduced to bringing together wagonloads of pretend 'plunder' and getting a group of Gauls to dress up as Germanic tribesmen. Fitted out to look the part in red-haired wigs and woad, they were even made to learn a few Germanic phrases so that the illusion of military success might be maintained.

In 39 C.E., Caligula outraged the Jews when he demanded that their temple be made over to the use of his imperial cult. His obstinacy came very close to triggering a major uprising before his client-king in the country, Herod Agrippa, managed to persuade him to change his plans.

GROWING OPPOSITION

One of Caligula's first actions as Emperor had been to bring to an end the political witch-hunt that had overshadowed the latter part of Tiberius' reign. The first months of his reign had indeed been a time of peace, but his illness had evidently changed all that. There was good reason for his paranoia. His sisters' plot with Lepidus apart, there were many with reason to want his overthrow.

And not just through personal ambition (although this was never in short supply in Rome). They would have been motivated, too, by a spirit of defending themselves. No one knew when Caligula was going to decide to feel slighted by some remark in the Senate or threatened by some political success, or when he would simply decide to contrive some phony prosecution so that he could seize someone's estate.

Inevitably, plots were hatched against this monster, but these succeeded only in making him more vigilant and more suspicious. Almost invariably, they were unsuccessful. Throughout 40 C.E., however, a conspiracy started to take form around the figure of Cassius Chaera, a tribune of the Praetorian Guard. So extensive was it that it managed to survive the official crackdowns. Try as they might, Caligula and his torturers could not get to everyone involved.

Cassius' resentment was largely personal. Although he was a big man and a war hero, he had a high voice,

which the Emperor had relentlessly teased him about, laughing and jeering at him and calling him a 'girl' before his men. Two senators assisted him. One was Annius Vinicianus, a friend of Lepidus who now feared for his life; the other was Valerius Asiaticus, one of those whose wife the Emperor had made free with, then taunted him with the fact thereafter. An unknown number of other individuals was involved.

A DRAMATIC FINALE

They decided to make their move at the opening of the Palatine Games on 17 January 41 C.E.: a wooden stage was built in front of the imperial palace for these

Given his taste for play-acting, it was appropriate that Caligula should have met his fate in a theatre: his assassination certainly made for a memorable scene.

festivities. The conspirators reasoned that, in the middle of all the noise and bustle, it should be relatively easy to isolate the Emperor from his bodyguards, especially if they waited in the narrow passageway he would have to make his way through when he left to take his lunch.

So it proved. Caligula, his minders straggling out behind him in the narrow passage, had stopped to talk to a group of young actors when Cassius Chaerea stepped forwards, drew a dagger and delivered the first blow. His comrades came up and stabbed the Emperor in their turn. Caligula was dead, but there was to be more bloodletting before the drama was done. In grief and rage, his bodyguards poured down the passage, swinging wildly about them with their swords. They killed a number of the conspirators, but in the violent confusion several innocent bystanders were cut down, too. Meanwhile, a separate group of assassins had stolen off to the imperial palace to murder Caesonia, the Emperor's fourth wife, and their infant daughter Julia Drusilla. They killed her by dashing her head against a wall. They would have killed his uncle Claudius, too (their aim was to destroy the Julio-Claudian Dynasty and restore the Republic), but loyal members of the Praetorian Guard took him into hiding.

III

THE IGNOMINIOUS EMPEROR CLAUDIUS

Gibbering, drooling and uncoordinated, Claudius cut a decidedly unimpressive figure. He ascended the throne determined that, while he might be despised, he would never be deposed. He rooted out conspiracies – real and imagined – with ruthless zeal.

✦

The soldier grabbed at the hanging with his left hand, readying himself with his right to ram his sword through whoever it was who was lurking behind. Minutes after the murder of Caligula, his guards were ransacking the playhouse in a fury, only too conscious that they themselves had been caught out. But enraged as he was, steely in his anger, the soldier still couldn't bring himself to strike the figure he found cowering behind the curtain. It was hardly even a man, more a gibbering, snivelling, quaking

Claudius' handicaps were most immediately apparent when he walked or talked; in repose he had a handsome face and a genuinely regal air. Not surprisingly, he tried as far as possible to have himself seen sitting quietly or standing still: that way he made a perfectly convincing Emperor.

heap. He grabbed it by the tunic and hauled it up into a standing position.

Before him, he realized with rising incredulity, was Claudius, Caligula's uncle, and with his nephew's death the new Emperor of Rome. The soldier called to his comrades. Conferring quickly, they ushered him away, and he was taken to a camp outside the city. It was ironic, but all too easy to believe that, as the assassins prepared the way for their attack on Caligula, they had chivvied Claudius away as just another member of the crowd. No one had seen him slip away in the noise and confusion that followed because, in abject terror, he went to find a place to hide. But then that was utterly typical of Claudius, the most mousy and nondescript of emperors and an object of his contemporaries' contempt.

Above: Claudius' contemporaries were no more able to overlook his difficulties than they were to understand them: they viewed him with abhorrence as an imbecile, a freak. In fact, the Emperor was a highly intelligent and capable man, the author of a highly regarded book on history.

REAL ACHIEVEMENTS

History has been a bit more respectful towards Tiberius Claudius Caesar Augustus, who ascended the imperial throne in 41 C.E. Within three years, he had swapped his inherited *agnomen* Germanicus for 'Britannicus', a title that was all his own. Not that the conquest of a windswept isle off the northern coast of Gaul amounted to so much in the imperial scheme, but it was nevertheless a genuine achievement. Julius Caesar's exploratory foray into Britannia had been repelled in 55 B.C.E., and the will had not been there until now to follow through. Claudius also added territories in the Balkans and the Middle East, and completed the conquest of Mauritania, begun under Caligula. A great builder of public works, he constructed important aqueducts and developed the port of Rome at Ostia. He undertook a major land-reclamation scheme around the

Right: Claudius was so thoroughly ridiculed in his own lifetime that it seems odd to see him depicted as a conquering hero. Yet he had better claims than many other emperors: it was in his reign that Britain was added to the Empire, along with several other territories.

Fucine Lake in central Italy. More than 30,000 men spent a decade digging a 3.5-mile (5.6km) tunnel through Monte Silviano to drain the area. He was a scholar of note (the eminent historian Livy had been his tutor as a teenager), and he wrote a highly regarded history of the wars against Carthage.

'A MONSTROUS SPECIMEN'

But Claudius had more fundamental challenges to contend with. From boyhood he had been sickly, and physically not entirely in control. His hands shook, he stammered, he had a tendency to drool and he lurched and limped in an awkward manner when he tried to

Below: Antonia Minor had many qualities, but compassion was not to the fore; nor did she have the imagination to appreciate the challenges her son faced. She did more than anyone else to brand the young Claudius a 'monstrous specimen', an acceptable butt for the cruel humour of the court.

V

CLAVDIVS CAES.

5

walk. He would burst out laughing, abruptly and unaccountably. He would fly into rages, spitting and slobbering as he raved.

> While Caligula took a savage delight in humiliating Claudius, with cruel put-downs and practical jokes, it never seems to have occurred to him to have Claudius killed.

Today, it is taken for granted that some deep underlying condition caused these problems, and Tourette's syndrome or cerebral palsy have been suggested. But these explanations were obviously not available to the Romans. To his family, it was an embarrassment that Claudius did not seem to know how to behave. Claudius' mother, Antonia, was Augustus' niece, the daughter of the first Emperor's sister, Octavia. She took the reputation of the imperial household very seriously. She despised the 'monstrous specimen' she had given birth to and, in hopes that some decorum might be beaten into him, had him tutored – even into adulthood – by a muleteer.

His perceived 'stupidity' almost certainly saved his life. Caligula had not been one to leave a likely rival alive, but no one had ever envisaged Claudius as Emperor. While Caligula took a savage delight in humiliating Claudius, with cruel put-downs and practical jokes, it never seems to have occurred to him to have Claudius

Claudius' third wife, Valeria Messalina, was a truly terrifying woman: murderous in her rages, insatiable in her lusts. Those who resisted her sexual advances or crossed her in any other way quickly found themselves paying for their temerity with their lives.

killed. He was openly disdained at the court. Far from being accorded the respect due to one of his rank and connections, it was all he could do to secure a place in the palace dining room. When he dropped off at dinner, which he sometimes did, aristocratic young nobles found it amusing to wake him by pelting him with olive stones.

A COWARD AND A KILLER

Hectored, put upon and bullied, it is hard not to feel for the young emperor-to-be; however, as Emperor, Claudius showed a less than pleasant side. He had a cruel streak. While other emperors endowed games and gladiatorial contests to please the people, Claudius was notorious for the extent to which he entered into the bloody spirit of shows where men and animals were tormented and killed. Contemporaries described him as being beside himself with excitement at these scenes of slaughter, joining in the cheering and shouting with the most raucous elements of the crowd.

It is understandable that Claudius should have been afraid of assassination, given recent Roman history (and his own experiences), but he took vigilance and caution to comic lengths. He wouldn't even eat at a banquet except under armed guard; if he went to visit a friend or relation who was ill, he had their chamber, even their sickbed, thoroughly checked over first.

He was dangerous in his timidity, though, and all too quick to see conspiracies. Claudius was utterly cold-blooded in removing potential threats. Although actually delighted at Caligula's death, he had Cassius Chaerea and other leading conspirators put to death as a long-term 'insurance policy' for his own protection. It didn't stop there. In all, he had more than 35 senators and 400 other patricians executed, often on very dubious grounds.

Inevitably, this irrational, panic-driven bloodlust made him the target of real conspiracies. One threat that certainly had

She may have a look of the Madonna about her, as seen here with her son Britannicus, but there was nothing virginal about Valeria Messalina. Nor was there anything mild and gentle: Messalina was responsible for many deaths, convincing Claudius that there were conspiracies all around.

not existed only in Claudius' imagination was the uprising of 42 C.E., which was led by Scribonianus, the Governor of Dalmatia. The rebellion won the support of several senators, but was savagely put down and another round of political executions ensued.

Those around the Emperor learned to play upon this aspect of their master's nature, especially his third wife, Valeria Messalina, and her hangers-on. They had only to hint to Claudius that they suspected someone's loyalty and that individual would very soon be dead. Gaius Appius Silanus was married to Messalina's mother when he upset the lustful Empress by spurning her sexual advances. Her counselor, Narcissus, then concocted a story about having had a dream in which he had witnessed Claudius being attacked and murdered by Silanus as he lay in bed. It went without saying that the unfortunate man was put to death. Decimus Valerius Asiaticus was denounced simply because Messalina coveted his villa with its famous gardens. It wasn't long before he had been compelled to commit suicide and she had taken these for herself.

LADIES' MAN

As far as his contemporaries were concerned, the great problem with Claudius was that, although ostensibly the ruler of the world, he did not have any authority in his own home. His contemporaries did not see Claudius' many liaisons with women as 'conquests' that enhanced his masculinity, but rather as marks of his own subjugation to the female sex.

Of the women in Claudius' life, not too much is known, at least for the early years. He was first betrothed to Aemilia Lepida until Augustus took against her parents in 8 C.E. Livia Medullina, to whom he next became engaged, apparently fell ill and died on the very day she was supposed to be marrying him, around 9 C.E. Almost immediately, Claudius married Plautia Urgulanilla. They had a son, Claudius Drusus, but he died young of some illness.

Urgulanilla bore a daughter, too, but it was an open secret that young Claudia was not Claudius's child, so he refused to recognize her as his. In 24 C.E., Claudius

divorced Urganilla on the grounds of her infidelities and the suspicion that she had conspired to murder her sister-in-law. Four years later, he married Aelia Paetina. He divorced her in 31 C.E. after the disgrace and death of Sejanus, her adoptive brother.

MESSALINA'S TRIUMPHS

If the available data on Claudius' earlier relationships with women is disappointingly scant, however, what we have on Valeria Messalina more than makes up the deficit. The Emperor's second cousin, whom he married in about 37 C.E., was rapidly to become an

Messalina's lusts were legendary: she had lovers by the score, it was said, and her behaviour made the Emperor even more a laughing-stock than he had been before. Ultimately, she was to pay for her ungovernable licentiousness with her life – her outrageous conduct could no longer be ignored.

anti-icon, a symbol of all that could be destructive in womanhood.

Messalina bore Claudius a son, Britannicus, who was born in 41 C.E. But that was about as much as she delivered in terms of her wifely duties. She could hardly have been less like the Empress figure as

WORKING GIRL

Juvenal, in his *Sixth Satire*, offers consolation to cuckolded commoners by bidding them attend the humiliations of even the highest born. 'Listen to what Claudius had to put up with,' the poet Juvenal tells his Roman readers:

The moment his wife saw her husband asleep, this exalted whore in her shamelessness opted for a bit of grubby matting over the imperial couch. Pulling a shawl on over her head, she stole out into the night, her black hair hidden beneath a lighter wig, and took herself off to work in a cheap bordello. She had her own little room there, where she waited at the ready, her nipples tricked out in gold, under the assumed name of Lycisca … Anyone who wanted her was welcome, as long as he paid his fee. The only problem was when the night shift was finally over. She never wanted to leave, and was eventually compelled to do so, full of disappointment, the desires burning inside her as strong as ever. Her body exhausted – but still unsated – she went back to her own bed, her face dirty from her couplings and from the smoke of the oil lamps, to foul her palace pillow with the brothel's smells.

Juvenal's *Satires* saw the civilization of Rome as being very much a veneer: beneath, he saw only evil and corruption. The rot started at the top, as far as he was concerned: at the very heart of the imperial household were hypocrisy, selfishness, cynicism and unbridled lust.

idealized in the memory of Livia Augusta. Messalina was completely out of control in her sexual desires. Her lovers were legion, the gossips said, and she was exhibitionistic in her lusts. There was more than a streak of sadism in her psychological make-up, too. Not content with being whorish herself, she used her authority as Empress to force other women to be unfaithful, often making them commit adulterous acts before the very eyes of their helpless husbands.

Her hold over Claudius was complete and ruthlessly exploited. She even manipulated him into using his imperial power against himself. In some cases, where men had resisted her advances, she persuaded her hapless husband that she needed their cooperation for some innocent purpose, but that they were unwilling. She made Claudius command them to do whatever she

Messalina saw herself as a priestess of passion, a servant of Bacchus, the god of wine and wanton lust. She finally brought about her own downfall when, moving beyond the casual affairs that were customary in Rome, she entered a sacrilegious parody of marriage with one lover, Silius.

demanded. When the required service turned out to be sexual, what else could they do but comply? Claudius was cuckolded by his own imperial order.

AN AFFAIR TOO FAR

It seems to have been around 47 C.E. that the Empress fixed on Gaius Silius as the object of her predatory affections. There is no great surprise here. Silius was a noble and a senator. More to the point, perhaps, he was celebrated for his good looks. That he was already married was hardly going to matter to Messalina. Nor did she care, at least initially, that he showed no sign of reciprocating her desires. Undaunted, she harassed his wife Junia Silana with threats until she was forced to leave her home, whereupon Messalina took possession of Silius herself.

At first he was shocked and terrified at what was happening, but he had little alternative but to give Messalina what she wanted. If he refused, he knew, she would find some way of contriving his death. He quickly succumbed, and was soon almost as involved in the affair as the Empress herself.

CARNAL COMPETITION

We owe to Pliny the Elder one of the most infamous anecdotes of Messalina's crazed immorality, the story of how she challenged Rome's leading prostitute to a sexual marathon. It occurs in his *Natural History*, where the episode is used to illustrate the author's theories on the differences between human sexuality and the instincts of the animal kingdom. Whereas the other animals want sex in season, Pliny says, humans are ready for it at any hour of the day or night, and, while the other animals are sated by sexual activity, humans almost never are.

Messalina, the wife of Claudius Caesar, seeing this prize as one worthy of an Empress' winning, chose to decide the question in competition with one of Rome's most notorious prostitutes. After continuous intercourse by night and by day, she triumphed at the twenty-fifth coitus.

She wanted to keep going, onlookers said.

One of the foremost ancient scientists, Pliny the Elder found in the Empress Valeria Messalina one of the animal kingdom's strangest specimens, but one who amply demonstrated one of his theories.

Almost, but not quite. It would have been hard for anyone, indeed, to be as engrossed as Messalina in what was becoming a wild fantasy of married life. She was entirely open in her visits to Silius' house and made herself at home there to the extent of bringing furnishings from the palace and staffing it with slaves from the imperial household.

SINISTER SCHEME

Time went on, and the Empress flaunted her adultery ever more openly. In secret, though, things had taken a still more sinister turn. The couple was contemplating making their union permanent, and removing Claudius entirely from the scene. If he were dead, they reasoned, they might themselves be the Empire's first couple, with Silius reigning as Emperor in Claudius' place. Silius, who had no children, would adopt Messalina's son Britannicus as his own. That way, Messalina could both have her lover and her son's succession, the two

overriding objects of her life. Messalina liked the scheme. But before she consented, she had to be sure that Silius was going to stand by her and wasn't just using her as his way to the imperial throne.

So it came about that, in public, in the presence of priests and witnesses, Messalina and Silius went through a solemn ceremony of marriage, despite the fact that both were already married, Messalina to the Emperor of Rome. It was a perfect parody of the real thing, even down to the blushes of the bride, a joyous wedding banquet and a romantic 'first night' for the couple afterwards.

Inevitably, these proceedings came to the Emperor's attention. Claudius could not overlook so spectacular an affront to his prestige, or so imminent a threat to his life. He sent word that the conspirators should be put to death. Even Claudius' advisers worried that the Emperor might let Messalina talk him round. No one was louder in his warnings than Narcissus, Messalina's

Scheming to the last, Messalina casts about for some escape from her inevitable end in this nineteenth-century French painting. She shrank from giving herself her death blow, as the Emperor had demanded. In the end, his messenger ran out of patience with her dithering. Snatching the weapon from her, he did it for her.

former ally. His advisers took the Emperor to Silius' house to see how thoroughly his wife had made herself (and his imperial possessions) at home there. Yet he still wavered, but in the end he allowed his death sentence to stand.

In deference to her rank, Messalina was offered the chance to deliver her own death wound. When she touched the chill blade to her breast, however, she flinched at its sharpness. She held it to her throat, but lowered her hand again. She tried her breast once more, but could not do what she had to do. In the end, the messenger who had brought her the sword grew tired of her hesitation. He took the weapon back from her and ran her through without compunction.

OUT OF THE FRYING PAN

Claudius appeared to have learned his lesson from his experience with Messalina. At one point, addressing the men of his Praetorian Guard, he admitted that his marriages had turned out so badly that he had no intention of getting himself hitched again. More than that, indeed, Claudius wanted them, if he showed any sign of weakening, to kill him on the spot with their own bare hands.

But Claudius was incapable of changing his nature. He was soon scouting around for a suitable woman to wed. In fairness, he was partly the victim of his advisers, who had clearly decided that it would be easier to control him through the offices of a wife. Negotiations were opened with his ex-wife Aelia

THE GARDENS OF LUCULLUS

The garden where Messalina met her end was no ordinary plot, but one of the most famous pleasure grounds of antiquity. It had been created in republican times, in about 60 B.C.E. by the famous general Lucius Licinius Lucullus on the Pincian Hill, on the northern edge of Rome. Fabulously rich after a string of conquests in Anatolia and Persia, Lucullus had come back and built a villa and a garden worthy of an eastern king. He had in fact been influenced by the gardens that he had seen in Mesopotamia and Persia.

Approached up a magnificent stairway, the garden was laid out along terraces, with exotic flowers and shrubs, its pathways punctuated by the finest of Greek sculptures. There were leafy trellises, picturesque grottoes, fountains and other water features. There were covered walkways, belvederes and miniature villas with stunning wall paintings and mosaic floors.

Strictly speaking, Roman generals and statesmen were not supposed to go in for this kind of oriental luxury, and it was no compliment when his contemporaries called Lucullus 'Xerxes in a Toga', after the ancient Persian emperor. One positive thing that can be said about the Gardens is that, compared with the rural complexes Lucullus had constructed in the south, near the Bay of Naples, at least the Roman retreat was extremely restrained. In the south, seawater was brought through tunnels dug through hillsides to fill fishponds, moats and bathing pools above which his various villas and summerhouses stood on stilts.

But Messalina loved the Gardens of Lucullus so much that she persuaded Claudius that their owner, Decimus Valerius Asiaticus, was conspiring against him, just so that she could get her own hands on them after he was forced to commit suicide. She spent many happy, if immoral, hours here in the years that followed, and it is probably fair to say that if she'd wanted to die anywhere it would have been here.

The gardens of the Villa Borghese offer a scene of heart-stopping beauty: the Gardens of Lucullus, on the same site, must have seemed just as idyllic in Messalina's day.

A LUST FOR POWER

In its sheer intensity and openness, Messalina's passion for Silius seems to go beyond the bounds of ordinary desire, tipping over into something more like insanity. Despite this, it has been suggested that there was dynastic method in her madness. Messalina had a master plan.

A match for the Empress in both shamelessness and ambition, Agrippina the Younger was by now back from her Pontine exile. Recalled after Caligula's death, the sometime pearl diver was appearing at spectacles with Lucius Domitius Ahenobarbus (later known as Nero), her son by her husband, Gnaeus Domitius Ahenobarbus. Mother and son alike had been a big hit with the Roman public.

As the boy was related to the ruling family through both his mother and his father Domitius, he posed a potential threat to Messalina's son, Germanicus. The Empress had, it was reported, already sent assassins to strangle Nero in his bedchamber. The would-be assassins had fled in fright, startled by the sight of a snake, beside his pillow. It turned out to be nothing more than a skin, shed harmlessly by a snake earlier that day. Agrippina had the snakeskin set in gold as a protective bracelet for the boy.

This consideration may have weighed as much with her as her lover's own mounting ambition in persuading her that Claudius should be murdered and Silius established in his place.

Paetina and with Lollia Paulina, who had for a few short months in 38 C.E. been married to Caligula).

But neither of these rival candidates was a match in cunning or ambition for Agrippina the Younger, Caligula's sister-mistress and Messalina's Nemesis. And while both Paetina and Paulina had their supporters at court, Agrippina had the ear – and, some contemporaries said, a great deal more – of Claudius' most trusted adviser, the Greek freedman Pallas, who was secretary to the Treasury.

> There was deep public hostility to the idea of his marrying Agrippina, but Claudius was by now besotted with his niece. He coaxed some of his senators into speaking up for the match, claiming that it was in the public interest.

Whether or not the two were lovers, Agrippina and Pallas certainly made a formidable team. Still, Agrippina's cause should have been a lost one from the start. She was, after all, the Emperor's niece. While the

Julio-Claudian Dynasty did like to keep power as far as possible 'within the family', this was going too far (or, rather, too close) by quite some way.

But Claudius wanted what he wanted. In attracting his attention, Agrippina had been able to take advantage of her kinship connection. This had given him access of a sort that would never have been allowed to another woman, and enabled her to give him 'cousinly' embraces that had left him wanting more. Few doubted Agrippina's ruthlessness. On her return from exile, on Claudius' orders she had married Crispus, an extremely wealthy man. He had died just a few years later. Tales were rife in Rome that he had been poisoned.

Claudius was persuaded by Paulina's backers not to take up with Paetina again: she would conclude that she was indispensable, and become overbearing. But Paulina herself was then charged with witchcraft on charges quite clearly manufactured by Agrippina. She was sent into exile and subsequently forced to commit suicide.

There was deep public hostility towards the idea of his marrying Agrippina, but Claudius was by now besotted with his niece. He coaxed some of his senators into speaking up for the match, claiming that it was in the public interest. And so, at the beginning of 49 C.E., the couple married and Agrippina the Younger became Empress.

AGRIPPINA IN CHARGE

Agrippina was every bit as domineering a wife as Messalina had been, but she was domineering in a very different way. Pride, rather than passion, was her vice, but she burned with as intense a lust for power as Messalina had for male flesh.

Even before marrying Claudius, she had been busily insinuating herself – and her son – ever closer to the central point of power in Rome. In 48 C.E. she had set her sights on Nero's marrying Claudius' daughter, Claudia Octavia. She was already betrothed to a young man of good family, Lucius Junius Silanus Torquatus, but Agrippina easily saw him off. She spread the story that Silanus was incestuously involved with his own sister. Claudius broke off the betrothal and dismissed Silanus from public office. In his shame, he committed suicide.

By now, though, Agrippina no longer needed to have Nero marry Octavia. As Empress herself, she was able to get Claudius to adopt him as his son. That left Nero as the obvious pretender to the throne. Britannicus might be Claudius' biological son, but his mother's disgrace had been so complete and so catastrophic that it was hard to see the Emperor naming him as his heir.

BELATED REGRETS

It was not long, however, before it became clear that Claudius was regretting his marriage to Agrippina. Worse, as far as she was concerned, he was leaning towards Britannicus in his affections. He was openly floating the idea of reinstating him as his heir. In his sixties now, and in failing health, Claudius was thinking about sorting out his affairs, including the succession. Did Agrippina feel that her hand was being forced?

Claudius had long been ailing when, some time in 53 C.E., he took an abrupt and dramatic turn for the worse. He had just eaten a bowl of mushrooms offered to him by his wife when he was suddenly gripped by convulsive spasms and collapsed. At first, it is said, he lost consciousness, but when, soon after

that, he came round once more, he vomited up the entire contents of his stomach.

At this point, apparently, he showed signs of slight improvement – ominous signs, as far as Agrippina was concerned. In desperation, she begged the Emperor's physician, Xenophon, for help. No one realized the kind of help she had in mind. The doctor had been plotting with the Empress from the start. He now took a long feather, and pushed it down Claudius' throat, explaining that vomiting seemed to have helped his sufferings so it should be encouraged. In fact, the plume had been dipped in a strong and swift-acting poison, which finished off the patient there and then.

And that was that. Claudius was dead. His grieving widow lost no time in making her move. Her son Nero was quickly hustled onto the throne.

Claudia Octavia had the dubious privilege of catching the Empress Agrippina's eye as the ideal bride for her son Nero. That Octavia was the youth's half-sister was no object to a woman who had herself married her uncle in the Emperor Claudius.

IV

NERO: 'WHAT AN ARTIST!'

Nero's reign brought Rome to a new low point: the young Emperor was utterly out of control, pulled this way and that by ungovernable – and unmentionable – passions. When, in 64 C.E., the Roman metropolis went up in flames, it seemed he had succeeded in dragging the Empire into the inferno.

◆

Nero was already a seasoned survivor when he became Emperor in October 54 C.E., despite the fact that he was still only 16. He had escaped assassination himself and – it was widely held – seen an emperor assassinated on his behalf. Others had been murdered, exiled and imprisoned to clear his path to the throne.

His parentage was unpromising. His father, Gnaeus Domitius Ahenobarbus, had been a minor monster, accused of a wide range of crimes and

Some contemporary accounts insisted that Nero had worked with might and main to save the city of Rome, but he will always be the Emperor who 'fiddled while Rome burned'. Whatever the historic facts, the story picked up on a real truth: Nero's near-total heedlessness and self-regard.

misdeeds. These ranged from treason through fraud and incest to careless driving. His mother we have met already. Agrippina had pretty much single-handedly steered her son to power, but she had done a great deal of damage in the process. Loathsome he may have been, but Gnaeus did have a wry sense of the ridiculous. When his friends congratulated him on the birth of his son, he replied that anything born to him and Agrippina was sure to be thoroughly unlikable and a calamity for the state.

It was a joke, of course, even if it was a bleak one, but it makes a sort of sense. Nero was very much the man his parents made him. This was due to his mother in particular, and not just because Gnaeus died when his son was only three, but also because Agrippina's was such an overwhelming personality. Born into violence

Agrippina the Younger had already shown herself a ruthless operator when she engineered her marriage with her kinsman Claudius: she was indefatigable in pursuit of power on her son's behalf. Or was it on her own? Nero clearly distrusted his mother as deeply as he needed her.

and paranoia, Nero was formed by his relationship with a crushingly dominant mother. In other words, he was a psychological disaster waiting to happen.

MOTHER'S BOY

Born in 37 C.E., Lucius Domitius Ahenobarbus had been renamed Nero Claudius Caesar Augustus Germanicus when Claudius adopted him in 50 C.E. How a boy just becoming a teenager felt about assuming a whole new identity we do not know. Perhaps it really didn't matter, because such transactions were routine in Roman patrician circles. In any case, the great influence on young Nero was his mother.

By the time he came to the throne, Nero was already married to his stepsister Claudia Octavia, the daughter of Claudius and Messalina. The match was advantageous in cementing his connection with the Julio-Claudian Dynasty. Like so much else in Nero's life, the marriage was his mother's work. Agrippina had been a bitter enemy of Messalina, of course, but with the succession at stake she was prepared to let bygones be bygones. As we have seen, she had broken Octavia's betrothal to Lucius Junius Silanus Torquatus by hinting at an incestuous attachment between him and his sister, Junia Calvina. It had then been easy enough for her to engineer Octavia's engagement to her son.

They were married in 53 C.E., the year before Nero's accession, and it appears to have been an unhappy union from the start, so much so that there are reports that he several times tried to strangle her. But then what chance did any wife have? There was a general feeling in Rome that the young Emperor and his mother were far too close – their relationship at best smothering, at worst downright incestuous. Some said that, when they had been journeying in a litter together, they emerged with their clothing rumpled and with suspicious stains. The gossip was that, when Agrippina had disapproved of Nero's infatuation with one young mistress, she had weaned him off it with sexual treats of her own. Scurrilous lies? Quite possibly, and yet it was widely noted that

Right: Cool, calm, commanding – Nero's marble bust has all the dignity that the living, breathing Emperor was so signally incapable of attaining. There is no hint of the man whose murderous passions and animalistic sexual practices dragged the office of emperor through the moral mire.

ARTISTIC EXCESSES

The single best-known 'fact' about Nero is that he 'fiddled while Rome burned', even though the violin was not to be invented for another millennium at least. It is true, though, that he was a music-lover. His chosen instrument was the lyre, but he also prided himself on his singing. So concerned was he to preserve this accomplishment that he kept a voice coach in constant attendance. He would not make his own speeches before the Senate or the army, but had them read by someone else. To perfect his voice still further, he spent hours a day doing the sort of exercises used by professional singers of the day.

> Accustomed to unstinting praise, Nero came to believe that he had extraordinary vocal gifts.

Lying on his back, he would hold a weight of lead on his chest, so as to enhance his breathing. He would make himself vomit to flush out his insides, and he insisted on competing in the city's regular music festivals. It went without saying that he always won. What judge would dare mark down an emperor, and especially one who was known to be so touchy?

Accustomed as he was to unstinting praise, Nero came to believe that he had extraordinary vocal gifts. This was despite the fact that, for all his efforts, his voice was actually weedy and wavering, and more likely to prompt laughter than genuine applause. No matter, he could always rely on the acclaim of a captive audience, quite literally, because no one was allowed to leave the auditorium when he was singing. Some women even ended up giving birth during his performances.

Whether he really 'fiddled while Rome burned' is a matter of debate, but there's no disputing Nero's love of all things musical, or the extremes to which he took these – and other – passions.

DRESSING TO SHOCK

By clean-cut Roman standards, Nero cut a rather foppish figure. He wore his hair long, the tresses curled around in a sort of beehive on his head. During a visit to 'metrosexual' Greece, he even let his hair hang down behind.

In Rome, the dress code for appearances in public was strict for patricians, and they were meant to wear a tunic with a long wool toga wrapped around it. Nero went out with his tunic unbelted, and with loose robes (designed for indoor wear) on top. Often, he wore scarves of various bright hues around his neck and went barefoot. The message was unmistakable. The Emperor was delivering a calculated affront to everyday decorum by dressing in a manner that he knew would be regarded as effeminate by those around him.

Nero chose one particular slave-girl concubine who bore a startling resemblance to his mother.

Agrippina would, in fairness, have loomed large in anybody's life. She was utterly determined and single-minded in her ambition. Her ruthlessness was remarkable even by Roman standards. She would stop at nothing to see her son proclaimed Emperor and herself established as the power behind the throne. As Nero began to feel more confident in his position, he was to find his mother's interference at first tiresome and finally intolerable, but still he found his emotional enslavement impossible to break.

OUT OF CONTROL

He may have been under his mother's thumb, but more generally Nero was out of control. Perhaps he was in rebellion against his destiny. Disguising himself in the cap of a freedman, he would escape the confines of the imperial palace in the dead of night and rampage through the city streets like a low-born hooligan, brawling in taverns or beating up people he found out late alone.

But it was in the sexual arena that Nero showed himself most uncontrollable. His liaisons with boys of the nobility and married women were just the start.

His actions were as extravagant as his desires were outrageous. He had one youth, Sporus, castrated in an attempt to turn him into a woman. He had him dressed in the gown and veil of a bride and went through a form of marriage with him, before parading round the city with him in a litter. He took his 'wife' through all the most public places, such as the markets and the forums, kissing and caressing him ostentatiously as he went. With another youth, Doryphorus, Nero was happy to reverse the roles. He now played the bride as his 'husband' sodomized him. To add to the excitement, he cried out in the manner of a young virgin being taken roughly for the first time.

> It was in the sexual arena that Nero showed himself most uncontrollable. His liaisons with boys of the nobility and married women were just the start.

When all the obvious human vices had been exhausted, he experimented with a more animalistic sexuality. He disguised himself in the fur of a predatory beast and hid in a 'den' before flinging himself at the intimate parts of male and female victims bound to wooden stakes at his mercy.

AN ALTERNATIVE AMOUR

The one woman who looks as though she might have had the emotional pull to free Nero from his mother's orbit was the freedwoman Claudia Acte. For a long time, she was for the young Emperor's closest female companion. He showered wealth upon her. In fact, researchers have found records of her property and she ended up a lady of some substance, with a large household, full of slaves, and three estates. More than this, though, Nero seems to have felt respect and even something close to reverence for her.

Another scolding for the boy-emperor who was never entirely to escape his mother's apron strings; their relationship was oppressively intense – even incestuous, it was whispered. Finally, Nero had Agrippina murdered, but this brought him no release; he was tortured by the enormity of what he had done.

Nero's love for Sporus was such that he had him castrated to make him more womanlike, then went through a form of marriage with him. His actions scandalized his own age, but they were to captivate nineteenth-century pornographers, who could offer titillation under the guise of 'history'.

Their sexual relationship was rooted in a deep and genuine emotional attachment. Although the liaison started in secret, it continued despite its discovery by Agrippina, who nearly went insane in her fury at finding herself with an uppity slave girl as a rival and, very nearly, as a daughter-in-law. Nero was so besotted with Acte that he made serious efforts to marry her. He even bribed officials to perjure themselves by swearing that she was really of royal birth. An emperor couldn't marry just anyone, of course, and least of all could he take a slave for his wife. Nero's officials, however, were ready to swear that Acte was descended from King Attalus of Pergamum, in Asia Minor, until Agrippina exposed the whole thing as a fraud.

The Prefect of the Praetorian Guard, Sextus Afranius Burrus, and Nero's tutor, Lucius Annaeus Seneca discreetly encouraged the relationship. Both hoped that the more involved the Emperor became in his affair with Acte, the less dependent he would become upon his mother. There were genuine concerns about the reaction of the people if vague gossip about incest in the imperial household were to be confirmed. What the legions would do if word got out did not bear thinking about. Even so, Seneca and Burrus were mainly motivated by political considerations closer to home because they feared

> Nero, furious, threatened Locusta with death if she did not come up with something that would work faster … she came up with another venom that she promised would be swift as a dagger.

Agrippina's over-dominance in the state. Nero felt much the same way and, passionate though his feelings for Acte evidently were, she was also a pawn in the power struggle between mother and son.

BROTHERLY LOVE

That struggle was eventually to become a fight to the death, as far as Nero was concerned. In the meantime, he had other scores to settle. His stepbrother, Britannicus, was still very young, but he had at very least as strong a claim to the throne as Nero did. Nero had every reason to wish him out of the way. Worse, Agrippina, having despaired of recovering her hold over her son, was now pushing Britannicus instead. Ultimately, she was determined to be the power behind the throne and, if it wasn't going to be Nero on the throne, Britannicus' would do just as well.

For the moment, an innocent boy of 13, Britannicus was oblivious to all this scheming, but it wasn't Nero's way to leave these things to chance. In 55 C.E., just a few days before his fourteenth birthday, Britannicus died suddenly after a seizure, the Emperor said. But after the first sudden shock of Britannicus' death, nobody really believed that. This was only too obviously the Emperor's crime.

Not that he hadn't had help. The poison used was the handiwork of Locusta, a woman held in high regard by those with an interest in murder and intrigue. She specialized in preparing subtle and slow-acting poisons, which mimicked the effects of naturally occurring illnesses. This one was given to the boy by his tutor, who was of course in the Emperor's pay. The toxin Locusta chose did not appear to work when first administered. Nero, furious, threatened her with death if she did not come up with something that would work faster, at which point she came up with another venom that she promised would be swift as a dagger.

Britannicus was dining with the imperial family and leading nobles when he was given the second

THE SHOWMAN

Nero's extravagance and frivolity, and his endless desire for fun and games of every kind, were almost as extreme as his depravity. Fancying himself both as a singer and as an actor, he spent huge sums endowing music and drama festivals and building auditoriums for dramas. He sponsored gladiatorial shows and sports events of every kind. He was a particular connoisseur of horseflesh and chariot racing. He himself once drove a team of 10 horses in an event at Olympia in Greece, and he would travel vast distances to attend the most minor race meetings.

Nero contends for the prize in person at the Circus Maximus in Rome: the Emperor was a devoted aficionado of horse and chariot racing.

Britannicus writhes in his death-agony, as re-enacted in the tragedy by the seventeenth-century French playwright Jean Racine. Offering as they did a potent cocktail of life, death, sex and power, Rome's imperial ups and downs were to prove a godsend for dramatists in more modern times.

poison, in a drink. So abruptly did it take him that he was unable either to speak or breathe. Instead, he collapsed before his horrified family and their guests. Nero stayed calm, telling the company that this was just an epileptic fit. The boy had always been prone to them, he said, and that story seems to have satisfied everyone, apart from Agrippina, an old hand at murder and conspiracy herself. She immediately guessed who was behind Britannicus' killing and she

> In 59 C.E., Nero, his patience now exhausted, began actively plotting his mother's death.

was also shrewd enough to work out that, as her son pursued his sinister strategy, she herself was almost certain to be next.

TAKING CARE OF MOTHER

Sure enough, in the months that followed, Nero consolidated his position by dismissing Burrus and Pallas (still treasury secretary) from theirs. He had them charged with treason, but Seneca intervened and defended them successfully. They escaped with their lives, but without the wealth and influence of old. Seneca, needless to say, saw his influence diminished after daring to make such a stand against his master. If these courtiers got off comparatively lightly, that seems to have been because Nero was saving all his hatred for his mother, with whom his conflict was intensifying all the time.

The final straw seems to have come in 58 C.E., when Agrippina tried to stop his relationship with Poppaea Sabina, who at the time was married to

A match for Agrippina in cunning and determination, Poppaea Sabina strengthened Nero's resolve, steeling him for the murder of his mother. She got her man, although the marriage does not appear to have been happy; Poppaea was ultimately killed by her husband during an argument.

Nero's friend Otho. Otho was destined to be emperor himself one day, but that was not known as yet. And besides, Poppaea was not the type to be kept waiting. She divorced Otho, the better to pursue her future with Nero. Agrippina remained obstructive. She was not prepared to see her son under another woman's thumb. And Nero's mood could hardly have been improved by the whispers that Agrippina hadn't given up her search for another puppet-emperor she could dominate. Now, it was said, she was plotting to have her son assassinated and replaced by her second cousin, Rubellius Plautus.

In 59 C.E., Nero, his patience now exhausted, began actively plotting his mother's death. His first efforts, it has to be said, suffered from a certain over-elaboration. He had skilled craftsmen modify the ceiling of Agrippina's bedchamber. They devised an ingenious mechanism by which it would suddenly collapse and kill her as she slept. But this was a

significant bit of engineering, involving considerable time and manpower, and it could hardly be concealed from someone as suspicious as Agrippina.

It had to be Plan B, then. This, too, was perhaps over-imaginative, involving a special self-sabotaging ship, which would suddenly start to fall apart once out at sea. It worked, as far as it went, sinking off the coast on its first voyage, but the sometime pearl diver simply swam to safety. Nero was in a fury when he heard the joyful tidings of his mother's survival. He had the

---

> ## Examining her tenderly all over, he horrified those present with his remark: 'I never knew I had such a beautiful mother.'

---

astonished messenger seized and put in chains. Thinking on his feet this time, he announced that the man had been an assassin sent by Agrippina to kill him. He sent his own men to deal with her. On his instructions, they left a dagger beside her body, so that it would look as though she had killed herself once her conspiracy had been uncovered.

A LOVER'S FAREWELL

Despite his part in her death, Nero was devastated by what had happened. Finally to be free of the woman who had dominated his life was emotionally overwhelming. Those emotions were hardly straightforward, though, and it was a lover's farewell that he paid her when he had her body stripped naked for his last viewing. Examining her tenderly all over, he horrified those present with his remark: 'I never knew I had such a beautiful mother'.

Yet the degree to which Nero felt liberated by Agrippina's death is evident in his public reaction. He clearly believed that he had won some great victory. And, just like a military conqueror, on his return to Rome he celebrated his achievement by processing

Locusta played a shadowy but crucial role in the darker history of first-century Rome: she was a specialist in death, a maker of the most sophisticated poisons. Here she tries out a new formula on an unfortunate slave: men like Nero were exacting clients.

through the streets before crowds of spectators in a
sort of triumph. He even offered the traditional
sacrifices on the steps of the Capitoline to thank the
gods for this latest victory they had granted Rome.

A SHORT WAY WITH WIVES

The way was now clear for Nero to offload Octavia
and wed Poppaea. Interestingly, though, he didn't
seem to be in quite such a hurry now. In 62 C.E.,
however, Poppaea capped the months and years of
unrelenting pressure with the revelation that she was
pregnant with his child. Nero duly divorced his wife,
saying that he would be sending her into exile on
charges of adultery.

No evidence was actually produced. One of
Octavia's maids was tortured to make her testify
against her mistress but would only tell her tormentor
that Octavia's private parts were purer than his mouth.
Even so, Octavia was exiled to Pandateria. No one
believed the accusations against her. After an
enormous public outcry, the Emperor was compelled
to bring her home to reinstate her as his wife.

There were scenes of general rejoicing, and
Poppaea's statues in the city were toppled, while
Claudia's were restored and bedecked with flowers.
Behind the scenes, however, Poppaea had been
persuasive. Nero agreed to have her rival killed.
Octavia was bound and her veins slit open so that her
death would look like suicide. In the event, her blood
clotted too quickly and she had to be killed by the
steam of a boiling bath.

Poppaea had her man. In 63 C.E. she was to bear
him a daughter, but Claudia Augusta died when only a
few months old. The Empress was expecting her
second child with Nero when, in 65 C.E., he came
home later than he had promised from the chariot
races. They had an argument, but what started as a
spat took a violent turn and he ended up kicking her
hard in the belly, the blow killing both Poppaea and
her child. (A son by her first husband, Rufrius
Crispinus, survived her: Nero would later have him
drowned 'accidentally' during a fishing trip.)

**Nero went over his mother's dead body as though it were a living
lover's, to the horror of all those who were looking on. Even in
death, he was unable to resolve his feelings for this woman who
had always overshadowed his life – and always would.**

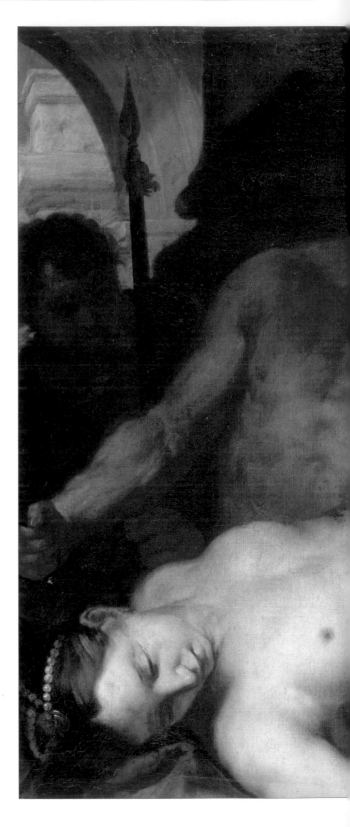

It is not clear whether Nero was already seeing Statilia Messalina by this time. She was certainly his mistress very soon after. That she was married was no obstacle to the ruler of the world. He had her husband Atticus Vestinus put to death so that she would be able to become his third wife.

INFERNO

But Nero had other things on his mind at this time apart from the ups and downs of his married life. In 64 C.E., a terrible fire had engulfed the heart of Rome. The middle of the city had been ablaze for six days and seven nights, its people forced to cower in the cemeteries, in their stone-built tombs. It was widely believed that Nero himself had been responsible because he had wanted to clear space for redevelopment projects – another of his vices. There were witnesses, well-regarded patricians, who claimed to have seen slaves leaving the palace with torches and kindling, but no one would have dreamt of detaining the Emperor's men.

It was a terrible conflagration. Of the city's 14 districts, only four emerged unscathed. Seven were gutted and three were completely razed. The urban fabric was vulnerable to big fires such as this. However grand their public buildings and palaces, when it came to ordinary residential architecture in their urban areas, the Romans took a 'build'em cheap and stack'em high' approach. Their *insulae* (literally 'islands') were towering tenement blocks, generally of wood construction, up to nine floors high, but often poorly built. With a tradesman's shop on the ground floor, and lower-cost rentals to be had on the floors above (the higher, the cheaper), a single *insula* might house as many as 40 people.

Hundreds are thought to have died in the inferno, and thousands more left homeless, their possessions lost. Crazed with fear and grief, some victims flung themselves into the flames. Others wandered aimlessly in bewilderment and shock. Bands of looters roamed the burning city, beating up anyone who tried to stop them.

Statilia Messalina was married when she became the Emperor's mistress: no problem – Nero had her husband executed so he could have her for his wife. Chilling ambition seems to have been one of the essential ingredients of femininity in the topmost echelons of Roman society.

Not that Nero was bothered. Notoriously, he went up to the palace roof, where the views were better, then sang, as he strummed cheerfully on his lyre. The song he performed, the 'Capture of Troy', commemorated another great city's destruction – not the most tasteful of choices.

It is only fair to be clear that the Roman historian Tacitus describes a completely different reaction on the Emperor's part. His Nero is as shocked as anyone by the fire. Out of town when the news of the outbreak reaches him, he rushes back to take charge of the rescue

> There were witnesses, well-regarded patricians, who claimed to have seen slaves leaving the palace with torches and kindling, but no one would have dreamt of detaining the Emperor's men.

and relief efforts. Tacitus derides the fiddler-on-the-roof story. He admits, though, that the tale was current. Because it was widely believed, he says, it badly hampered Nero's attempts to deal with the disaster.

AFTER THE FIRE, THE FOLLY

It hardly helped that, with the embers still glowing, Nero imposed high taxes on the city and the provinces to fund his reconstruction work. It also, of course, seemed to confirm the theory that the Emperor had arranged the whole thing, especially as he now proceeded to build himself a splendid residence. This was the *Domus Aurea* or 'Golden House', which was to be part-palace, part-country villa set in central Rome.

It was a truly monumental folly, the insanity starting in the vast vestibule with a colossal statue of Nero himself. Behind a triple colonnade well over half a mile long was a complex of buildings. These were laid out in the form of miniature cities, clustered around a lake made up with sandy shores and inlets like a sea. It was a little world: there were areas of open parkland, pasture and woodland groves; there were vineyards and cultivated fields. Inside, the buildings were bedecked with gold and jewels. The main hall for banquets had a revolving dome which made the light

change constantly, while special spouts sent flowers and perfume raining gently down upon the diners.

And what was Nero's reaction when this wonderland was ready for occupation? It would allow him to live like a human being at last, he said. It is hardly surprising that the *Domus Aurea* was controversial. So much so that subsequent emperors did not care – indeed, did not dare – to occupy it. Its valuable contents removed, the shell was abandoned and allowed to decay. The complex was demolished and the site built on top of a few years later.

> The revolt of the Britons under Boudicca in 60 C.E., for example, had felt like some kind of warning. But it was at home that Nero was feeling most badly beleaguered. There, in 65 C.E., Gaius Calpurnius Piso organized a major plot.

The scale of this self-indulgence inevitably overshadowed Nero's more intelligent reconstruction work in Rome. He rebuilt the residential districts destroyed by the fire along new and more rational lines, with wider streets to prevent or slow the spread of fire. Buildings were of brick construction, had spaces between them and were built to a restricted height. Covered colonnades at street level would not only offer pedestrians shelter from the rain, but their roofs would provide a platform useful in fighting future fires.

UNDER PRESSURE

There had for some time now been a sense that infernos were liable to break out in Nero's empire. The revolt of the Britons under Boudicca in 60 C.E., for example, had felt like some kind of warning. But it was at home that Nero was feeling most badly beleaguered. There, in 65 C.E., Gaius Calpurnius Piso organized a

The great fire of Rome, in 64 C.E., brought devastation to the Empire's capital – and to Nero's reputation. Even though he rebuilt the city afterwards, his subjects were deeply cynical about his motives: it was widely believed that the Emperor himself had contrived the conflagration.

Some chroniclers denied the claims that Nero had 'fiddled while Rome burned', but the accusation stuck, and he was never to be forgiven. It seemed in keeping with the Emperor's general indifference to the lives and concerns of his ordinary subjects.

major plot. The 'Pisonian Conspiracy', as it became known, involved as many as 19 senators and several other leading citizens. The plan was to kill Nero and replace him with Piso.

The plot came to nothing, in the sense that it came to light through an informant. Even so it shook the state to its foundation. No fewer than 41 individuals (including four women) were executed, and many more were exiled. Nero's old tutor Seneca, who had been a thorn in the Emperor's flesh for some time now, was ordered to commit suicide.

REBELLION AND DISCONTENT

The pressure on Nero continued to mount. There was an insurrection in Judea in 66 C.E., then another in Gaul the following year. Although the Jewish Revolt was serious – and would not ultimately be put down

until after Nero's death – the unrest in Gaul was still more disturbing. This was because it was a rebellion by Romans, led by the local governor, Vindex, a reaction to the taxes imposed by the Emperor in the aftermath of the Great Fire. Galba, the Governor of Hispania, rose up in support.

> Nero's old tutor, Seneca, who had been a thorn in the Emperor's flesh for some time now, was ordered to commit suicide.

Insignificant in itself, the rebellion was put down with relative ease. The problem was that it had highlighted a more general discontent across the Empire. Hostile factions within Rome started agitating openly against Nero, and, in June 68 C.E., a Senate vote declared him a public enemy. Galba was proclaimed Emperor in his place.

VIOLATING THE PROPRIETIES

Vast banquets were held on an artificial island in the middle of the lake at the *Domus Aurea*. The dining couches were arranged around a central platform, with temporary structures serving as mock-'taverns' and 'brothels' arrayed around. The guests could come and go at will between the tables and the taverns, and any time they felt like it they could pay a visit to one of the brothels.

There some of the city's most aristocratic virgins and wives were to be found, along with the capital's most glamorous courtesans. However respectable, they were under orders not to turn down any approach on pain of death. A more outrageous affront to the social proprieties can hardly be imagined, especially because there were male slaves among the Emperor's guests, allowed to have their pick of the patrician women. Senators and consuls could only look on helplessly as their wives were raped, their daughters deflowered by slaves and gladiators.

In the Domus Aurea, Nero could entertain on an unprecedented scale, setting new standards in extravagance and immorality. These orgies made prostitutes of the Empire's noblest women, corroding the civic and social fabric, and finally threatening the stability of the state.

EMPEROR AND ANTICHRIST

Claudius is believed to have been concerned about the small but growing Christian community in Rome, but it was Nero who organized the first real crackdowns. It was he who brought about the martyrdom of Saints Peter and Paul. The Emperor's guards rounded up scores of Christians and, while some were thrown to savage dogs to be torn apart, others were nailed on crosses or burned in fires. So small a sect could hardly have been seen as a real religious threat to Rome, but it suited Nero to scapegoat the Christians for his own reasons. His claims that they had been responsible for the Great Fire of Rome in 64 C.E. helped distract public attention from suspicions that he himself had been to blame.

As a wave of similar persecutions drove the Christians underground, they communicated secretly using a code based on *gematria*. At its most exalted level, this was a numerological theory exploring the relations between the Hebrew language and number systems, and it provided the basis for a code. For Nero, the figures came to 666: the 'Number of the Beast' in the Book of Revelation. Many early Christians did indeed see the Emperor Nero as a reincarnation of the Antichrist.

Depicted here by Caravaggio, St Peter was crucified – upside-down – in Rome. For the moment, at least, the new Christian religion had comparatively few adherents – but it made a convenient scapegoat in times of stress.

Nero fled and, realizing that the end was inevitable, prepared to kill himself. He asked his friends to dig a grave for him and make ready what they would need to deal with his dead body. It wasn't quite the 'Roman death' of heroic tradition. Nero was physically timorous, and frightened to proceed when the moment came. Indeed, he was on the brink of thinking better of the whole idea when he heard that his enemy was quickly closing in. He asked his friends what fate awaited him in his captors' hands. They told him that

he could expect to be stripped naked, pinned down and beaten to death with rods. Anything rather than that, Nero concluded.

Even now, though, he could not bring himself to deliver the final blow. In the end his secretary Epaphroditos had to help him. He was only just in time. Bursting in to arrest him, the Praetorian guardsmen saw Nero departing from this life. He died, as he had lived, a man of immense pretensions: his final words were, 'What an artist dies in me!'

AN ECCENTRIC AFTERLIFE

That was not quite the end. If Rome's political elite were overjoyed to see him go, the ordinary people were desolate at his loss. Messy as his private life had been, Nero had been a great endower of games and shows, so the mass mourning that followed his death was quite sincere.

> Even now, though, Nero could not bring himself to deliver the final blow. In the end his secretary Epaphroditos had to help him.

And he was missed all the more as time went on. Given that his death was followed by several years of instability, that is perhaps not so surprising. Certainly, it was not long before people were looking back nostalgically to a reign that most had experienced as a time of prosperity and peace. Some even went so far as to believe that Nero would come back from the dead as deliverer of the Empire.

This view was especially strong in the east, where the tradition of worshipping emperors as gods was widespread. A number of reincarnations were claimed. One lyre-playing lookalike turned up in 69 C.E., and he very nearly succeeded in persuading the Parthians to start another war. Another emerged around 80 C.E., during Titus' reign when the Romans' eastern frontier was unsettled throughout this period. And then finally, some 10 years after that, a third pretender appeared, claiming to be Nero, bringing about a full-scale rising in the east.

IN THE STEPS OF THE CAESARS

After the insanity of 69 – the 'Year of the Four Emperors' – the reigns of Vespasian and Titus brought a welcome period of stability. It was the calm before the storm: Domitian was a man tormented by paranoia and driven by demented – often sadistic – urges.

◆

The Julio-Claudian Dynasty died with Nero. Its existence had hardly been a source of political stability, but its absence was a guarantee of chaos. The imperial throne was up for grabs, and there would have been no shortage of ambitious candidates, even if Nero's passing had been less messy.

As it was, Galba was barely on the throne before it became clear that he had fatally compromised his rule. Returning to Rome in triumph with his generals, he had demanded tribute in all the cities through which he passed. That was just storing up trouble for his new

Otho proved adept in seizing power, buying the backing of the Praetorian Guard. Staying there, however, was another matter. He was quickly toppled by Vitellius – not until the reign of Vespasian (above) was the Empire to experience a period of calm.

regime. And then, having upset these provincial (but often influential) communities, he next proceeded to alienate his own men. Once he was safely established in the capital, Galba decided he was no longer dependent on his legions. He might just as well keep for himself all the tribute his troops had raised. Why, he asked high-mindedly, should soldiers be bribed into loyalty to the Emperor when they were under oath to support him in any case?

GALBA GETS IT WRONG
It was a logical argument, perhaps, but it showed no understanding of human nature. His misreading of the situation in Rome was catastrophic, and Galba did not exactly strengthen his position by his puritanical insistence that he wasn't going to squander public

Galba's aspect was severe: he made much of his high-mindedness, but was suspected – rightly – of hypocrisy and greed. The result was that he could find little support from either his army or the Roman people when rival claimants rose up against his reign.

money on silly shows and spectacles. Over centuries, Romans had learned to look on such entertainments as their right, so Galba's attitude was viewed as stingy and mean-spirited.

LEGIONS REVOLT

Meanwhile, there was growing anger among the legions in Germania. They had refused to join in the mutiny with those in Gaul and Spain. Their reward for their loyalty, as far as they could tell, was that they were missing out on their share of the booty, which they were convinced the rebellious legions were getting. Worse, they found themselves regarded with suspicion by Galba's new regime precisely because they had stayed at their posts and done their duty!

Vitellius did not have much time to enjoy his imperial power. Having overthrown Otho, he was brought down in his turn just eight months later. Vespasian was clearly the coming man: so much of the army had rallied around him that Vitellius' own soldiers threw in their lot with him.

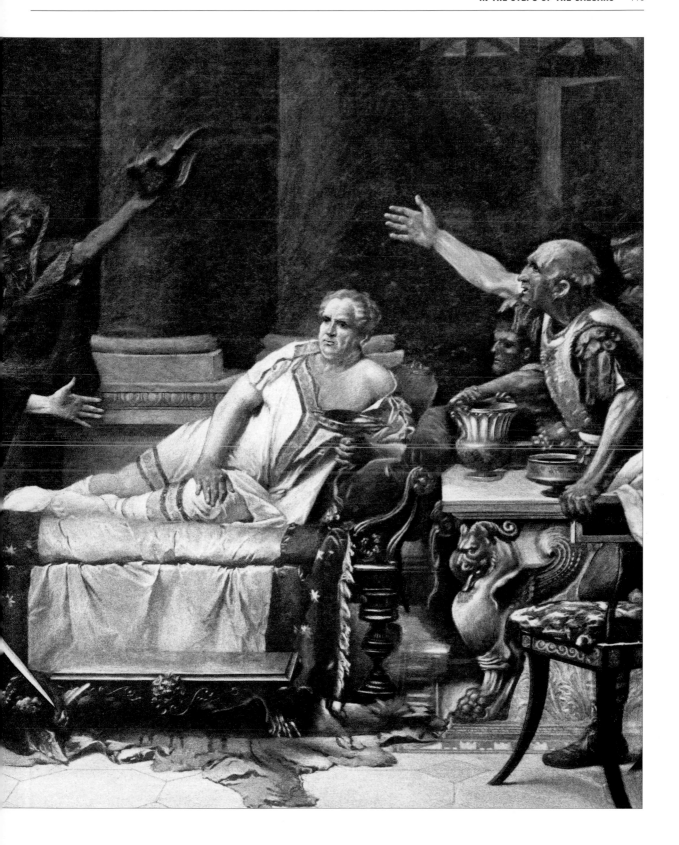

They proclaimed their own emperor, Vitellius, the Governor of Germania. The news sent shockwaves through the entire political system. With Rome in turmoil, Nero's old friend Marcus Salvius Otho was able to make a deal with the Praetorian Guard. Its senior officers were well bribed, this élite force marched into the heart of the capital with Otho. They assassinated Galba and acclaimed Otho as Emperor.

OTHO GETS IT RIGHT

That was on 15 January, but Otho was already reigning on borrowed time, even though he got things off to a promising start. He showed his rejection of Galba's penny-pinching ways by richly rewarding the soldiers and officials who had helped him. He also treated the people to lavish gladiatorial games. By adopting the additional name 'Nero', he made his intention of carrying on in this bountiful vein very clear. (Nero had been famous for his generosity in providing spectacles.) Rome decided that it liked its new Emperor, but it had few illusions about his motives.

Even as Otho took office, the German legions were advancing on Rome. They were bent on toppling Otho and installing their commander, Vitellius, on the throne. Defeated at the First Battle of Bedriacum, in northern Italy, Otho committed suicide. Only his death, he said, would save the Roman Empire from civil war. No one, in all honesty, would have expected such noble sentiments from Otho. In fact, some of his guards were so moved that they threw themselves onto his funeral pyre.

VITELLIUS AND VESPASIAN

Vitellius' vice was gluttony. He was vast in size, and said to gorge on extravagant banquets up to four times a day. At one such feast 2000 fish and 4000 fowl were served up to astonished guests. He was fastidious in his tastes, with a special passion for pike livers, partridge brain and flamingo tongue, and would send out naval ships to fetch these delicacies for his table.

Vitellius ascended a (presumably creaking) throne on 16 April 69 C.E. Meanwhile, the legions in the Middle East had been getting restless. They had come

Even the official sculptor sees little point in beating about the bush: Vitellius was a heroic gourmandizer, and it showed. Out of his depth as Emperor, he was to reign for only eight months before Vespasian arrived to eject him from his throne.

to the conclusion that they too had been missing out on the great political free-for-all. They proclaimed their general, Titus Flavius Vespianus ('Vespasian'), Emperor in the middle of July. While Vitellius was officially Emperor, he could read the writing on the wall, and it was clear how strong Vespasian's position was. It wasn't just the troops from the Middle East who had thrown their might behind his claim. All those legions that hadn't yet had their part of what they all seem to have seen as some great share-out of political power and plunder rallied to Vespasian's banner. Along with the troops from Judaea and the Parthian frontier, he had armies from Dalmatia and Asia Minor (modern Turkey). Faced with such odds, Vitellius' own forces had begun deserting in their droves. As Vespasian's strength grew, Vittelius's was dwindling fast.

> Vitellius was fastidious in his tastes, with a special passion for pike-livers, partridge brain and flamingo tongue, and would send out naval ships to fetch these delicacies for his table.

Vitellius would have been happy to surrender, but his supporters refused to let him back down. As the new Emperor, Vitellius had appointed his friends to key offices, especially in the Praetorian Guard, and they were obviously going to lose these positions if he fell. They more or less forced him into action at the Second Battle of Bedriacum. Vespasian was still in the Middle East when his troops met Vitellius' army here on 24 October 69 C.E. Vitellius' men gave a good account of themselves in a fight that continued through the night, but eventually they were beaten and put to flight.

Vitellius made his way back to Rome, where he lay low. He was discovered, though, and dragged out of his hiding place. Vespasian's men had him strangled as a traitor and thrown down the Gemonian Steps. The way was clear for their commander to return to Rome as Emperor. He was formally enthroned on 26 December, and he was destined to become the founding emperor of the Flavian Dynasty.

Above: A medieval artist imagines the scene in 69 C.E. when Vespasian's army arrived to topple Vitellius. At least, after all these tumults, Vespasian brought a period of peace and stability: he has little to contribute to a 'dark history' of ancient Rome.

Left: A plain-dealing, unpretentious soldier, Vespasian was the strongman needed to put the Roman world to rights in 69 C.E. His 10-year reign would be remembered as a time of discipline and order in an empire that had known all too little of either for some time past.

In the centuries since, the year 69 C.E. has become known as the 'Year of the Four Emperors': Galba, Otho, Vitellius and Vespasian. After this crazy time, however, Vespasian's reign was to provide a most welcome period of peace and calm. He poses something of a challenge to a 'dark history' of the Roman Emperors, so likeable was he and so comparatively blameless was his life.

been strong and genuinely devoted.

Domitilla died some time before Vespasian became Emperor. When that happened, he kept faith with his mistress, Caenis, a slave-woman. Although he couldn't marry her, she was to all intents and purposes his wife. She had started out as his secretary, and continued to assist him as Emperor, becoming his administrative right hand. There

A BIT OF PEACE AND QUIET

Until now, the nearest Vespasian had come to controversy was when he had fallen asleep during one of Nero's singing performances, an offence for which he had paid by being banished from the Emperor's inner circle. He had retired to the provinces in obscurity, but his military abilities had been too valuable to be allowed to go to waste for long. Soon he had been reinstated in the Roman establishment. Vespasian loved his wife, Flavia Domitilla. It's true that he had a mistress too, but their marriage seems to have

Right: Titus' boyish looks belie his uncompromising, even ruthless nature: he was indefatigable in tracking down traitors and suppressing sedition. His legendary drinking bouts and sexual exploits also suggest a driven, compulsive side – psychological demons the nature of which we can scarcely guess.

Following page: The Arch of Titus was erected in Rome to commemorate the young Emperor's conquest of Judaea in 70 C.E. As the Jews could testify – those who had survived his atrocities, at least – he had proven himself an immensely able military commander.

TOUGH TITUS

The Jews were not quite as fond of Titus as the Roman people were. It was he who had led the bloody assault that finally put down their four-year uprising in the summer of 70 C.E. He tried to terrorize the Jews into submission by massacring whole communities. He subjected the city of Jerusalem to a lengthy and unrelenting siege. Anyone found escaping or venturing forth to attack was captured and crucified on one of the hillsides overlooking the city. Soon there were tens of thousands of crosses there as an advertisement of Roman cruelty. When the breakthrough came, in August 70 C.E., Titus' troops roared through the city, slaughtering and setting fires as they went. The Temple was destroyed and all its treasures taken. All in all, Titus' armies had slaughtered a million Jews.

The rebels had been comprehensively defeated now, and Titus returned to Rome in triumph, but a diehard group was still holding out in the southern desert. Lucius Flavius Silva, the new Roman commander, hunted them down and finally cornered them in the mountaintop fortress of Masada. Their position appeared to be impregnable, but Silva's soldiers got to work and built a huge ramp of stones and soil up the sheer sides of the mountain. Once this was in place they were able to bring up big battering rams. In August 73 C.E., they smashed through the walls and found their way into the fortress. There they found that the 936 people inside – men, women and children – had committed mass suicide rather than fall into Roman hands.

Masada was the scene for one of history's most heroic last stands, when Jewish rebels committed suicide after a lengthy siege. A tragic chapter in the history of the Jews, for the Roman army this was business as usual, another triumph for Titus' all-conquering legions.

was a great deal to do. The morale of the army and the finances of the Empire had both been badly damaged by the months of anarchy before Vespasian came to power. As Emperor, he worked hard to restore these, and did so with considerable success. His death in 79 C.E. was widely mourned. The fact that he had died of natural causes would have been a shock in itself a few years before.

> Titus' legendary drinking bouts with friends were so infamous that many had doubts about his fitness for the throne. In the end, though, this early reputation only enhanced the positive impact he made when he came to power.

His son and successor, Titus, was to rule for just two years. He, too, impressed with his conscientiousness and administrative efficiency. He had served a sort of apprenticeship under Vespasian, taking charge of what we would today call 'internal security'. He had a rough way with dissent. Those he deemed traitors were often executed on the spot. When he got wind of a plot by Aulus Caecina Alienus to topple Vespasian, Titus invited him to dinner. Instead of serving him a meal, however, he had him stabbed to death.

ANOTHER EASTERN QUEEN

The young Titus was wild. His legendary drinking bouts with friends were so infamous that many had doubts about his fitness for the throne. In the end, though, this early reputation only enhanced the positive impact he made when he came to power. Once in office, he sobered up and impressed everyone with his administrative and political capabilities.

Titus' soldiers took no prisoners when they swept into Jerusalem in 70 C.E., killing, burning and destroying as they went. It wasn't driven by personal motivations – still less was the attackers' violence racially motivated – but it had to be shown that resistance to the Romans didn't pay.

The beautiful Berenice, Queen of Cilicia, became Titus' mistress in Judaea. For a time, indeed, he took her back to Rome. He later sent her away in deference to anti-foreign feeling in the Empire's capital, although he may have been hoping to bring her back after a decent interval.

The contrast with his earlier rowdiness and heavy drinking was astonishing.

Titus' romantic life had also attracted a good deal of negative attention, not so much because of the slave-girls or the boys, but rather for his long-term liaison with the Jewish Queen Berenice of Cilicia. The Romans weren't anti-Semitic as such, but they viewed all aliens as inherently suspicious. Berenice was another Cleopatra. Like the Egyptian queen, moreover, she was stalked by the phantom of incest. But Cleopatra's marriage to Ptolemy XIII had been a matter of dynastic tradition, and quite possibly never consummated. Berenice and her brother Agrippa II were said to have been head-over-heels in love.

This doesn't seem to have worried Titus, who met Berenice during his time in Judaea and made her his mistress. He sent for her when he later went back to Rome. Once he was named as Emperor, though, he bowed to popular opinion by dropping Berenice and sending her away. Titus was no romantic, then, but he was realistic in recognizing what was expected of an emperor. He may have just been going through the motions, too. It is highly possible he was hoping to bring Berenice back once he was more firmly established in his authority. However, he died in 81 C.E., only two years into his reign.

GOOD EMPEROR, BAD LUCK
Titus had made himself a model emperor, as far as the Romans were concerned. The great calamities of his brief reign were not his doing. He could hardly have been blamed for the catastrophic eruption of Mount Vesuvius, in August 79 C.E., which brought about the destruction of surrounding villages and towns. On the contrary, he won admiration for the speed and humanity of his response. He organized effective emergency relief for those communities that had suffered. Neither would anyone have dreamt of suspecting him of responsibility for another huge fire, which tore through Rome in 80 C.E., destroying several important public buildings, or the plague that struck the city at much the same time.

Like his father, Titus died in bed – again, apparently of natural causes – although there were reports that his younger brother Domitian had been plotting against him. The Emperor, in his big-hearted naïvety, was told of his brother's treachery, but refused to take any action against him. As he lay dying, though, he said that the one great regret of his reign was his refusal to listen and his failure to have Domitian done away with. In fact, there is no real evidence that Domitian played any part in Titus' death.

> Domitian's reign was to be remembered above all for its insane capriciousness and cruelty. He was regarded with absolute loathing and utter terror.

If Domitian were innocent of killing off Titus, it would be the last thing he was to be innocent of for quite some time. His reign was to be remembered above all for its insane capriciousness and cruelty. He was regarded with absolute loathing and utter terror.

A SPOILED CHILD
Evil like Domitian's isn't easily accounted for, but his upbringing was obviously different from his elder brother's in key respects. He was many years younger than Titus, and his mother had died when he was a small child. He had spent a great deal of time in his own company, alone with his thoughts and fantasies. While Titus had been given a role both in the army and the administration, Domitian had been left in idleness.

He hadn't been expected ever to be Emperor. In fact, he would not have succeeded his brother if Titus had not died unexpectedly at the age of 41. Domitian was bright and well educated, but had never had to take real responsibility, political or military. He was, however, used to having his own way.

He was in his twentieth year when, in 70 C.E., he met Domitia Longina, daughter of the consul Gnaeus Domitius Corbulo. She was married to a distinguished senator. Although Domitian had already had lots of affairs by now, he was so obsessed with Domitia that he had her forced to divorce her husband to marry him. Their marriage appears to have been successful for

When Vesuvius erupted in August 79 C.E., the sky was darkened by huge, thick clouds of ash which then drifted down, a hard, dry snow. Large areas were engulfed, including the cities of Pompeii and Herculaneum, the whereabouts of which were lost for centuries.

POMPEII FOR PLEASURE-SEEKERS

When Vesuvius erupted on 24 August 79 C.E., it sent hot ash in huge quantities high into the sky. This then cascaded down across an extensive area. Anything that lay below was buried beneath a thick, impenetrable blanket. This included two whole cities, Pompeii and Herculaneum. People, buildings, streets – all were famously lost, only to be rediscovered in more recent times.

Antiquarians who began digging up Pompeii in earnest in the late eighteenth century were stunned to find a city frozen in a single instant of the distant past. Miraculously preserved beneath ash and pumice were shops and taverns, a forum, streets, auditoria and houses. Several of these were richly decorated inside, with stunning frescoes and beautiful sculptures and ceramics.

As the excavations continued, however, researchers realized they were finding more than they had bargained for. The city had seemingly been obsessed with sex. The divinity of choice for the Pompeiians had apparently been Priapus, the god of lust. His statue, with its oversized phallus, turned up everywhere. Several of the buildings they investigated appeared to have been brothels, and their walls were painted with explicit erotic scenes. In Roman times, brothels were known as *Lupanares*

Frescoes in Pompeii's brothels helped create a mood of easy eroticism and advertised the sort of services that were on offer to their clients. The discovery of such pictures confirmed the view, already formed from written sources, that prostitution played an important part in Roman life.

(from the word *lupa* ('she-wolf'), slang for prostitute). Some of the frescoes they found, the antiquarians hastily painted over again, so embarrassed were they at what they had revealed.

The name 'Lupanar' is now generally reserved for the largest of these brothels in Pompeii. This had 10 rooms, several of them decorated with erotic paintings. Further frescoes have been discovered in some of the city's baths, and recent finds have included a lesbian scene.

some years, although definitely not conducted along conventional lines. Domitia spoiled him. Far from resenting her husband's mistresses, she was only too happy for him to have his fun, and would on occasion even join in threesomes with Domitian and his lovers.

AN INTERFERING EMPEROR

It did not take Domitian long to show himself completely out of his depth as Emperor. Not because he couldn't take charge, although, but because he

wouldn't stop meddling. Where other emperors had been happy to get on with their political intriguing and their debaucheries, Domitian wanted to interfere in every aspect of the running of the state. His officials

Right: Domitian built not one but two spectacular palaces on the Palatine Hill in Rome. The Flavian Palace was reserved for official functions. The Domus Augustana, shown here, was an architectural indulgence on a massive scale, a sumptuous residence in which Domitian could live in luxury.

never had a moment's peace. Even generals in the field and governors in faraway provinces received a steady stream of messages, orders and advice.

It was Domitian's tinkering with the economy that was to be most damaging, though. He began, soon after his accession, by raising the silver content of the denarius, the basic Roman coin, by about 12 percent. It was quite impossible to sustain this level. The economy of the Empire virtually ground to a halt, and, by 85 C.E., Domitian had been forced to devalue the currency. He attempted to boost grain production by introducing measures to restrict the cultivation of vines. These provoked enormous controversy and were so hopelessly impractical that they were never actually implemented.

> Even in public carnage, Domitian's tastes were warped. He even introduced clashes to the death between female gladiators and fighting dwarves.

In the end, though, Domitian gained popularity, not as an able administrator of the Empire but, like other Emperors before him, as a lavish provider of public shows. He was an enthusiast himself. He particularly loved mock battles, staging life-and-death contests between infantry and cavalry units, and built a new *naumachia* (a special amphitheatre), with a flooded arena for naval battles. Even in public carnage, Domitian's tastes were warped. He even introduced clashes to the death between female gladiators and fighting dwarves.

POPULAR GENEROSITY

To begin with, at least, the army looked at Domitian askance. He might be Vespasian's son and Titus' brother, but he hadn't seen any significant military service himself. Try as they might, they couldn't see him as one of their own. Again, Domitian had the ideal solution: throw money at the problem. He ramped up military spending and specifically soldiers' pay, and ended up being very popular with the troops.

Domitian splashed out on architectural projects, too. He built a splendid new Flavian Palace on the Palatine Hill for state functions. For purely domestic purposes, he constructed the extravagantly appointed Domus Augustana, just to the south. In keeping with his great hobby, he had this residence connected with the Circus Maximus by a special passage so he could come and go freely to its gladiatorial shows. He also had the famous amphitheatre enlarged. The fact is that he could fine-tune the economy as much as he liked but as long as he went on spending money like this, the Empire was facing ruin.

A DOUBLE STANDARD

In 85 C.E., Domitian had himself appointed *censor perpetuus* (censor for life). That gave him responsibility for supervising every aspect of moral life in Rome and a right to pry into whomever's affairs he chose. No emperor had done this before, but Domitian was such a notorious busybody that the decision didn't really come as a great surprise. No error was too insignificant to be worthy of his attention. He introduced a new law dictating that patrician ladies who had committed adultery could not be carried in litters through the city but had to walk, like common women. He was so outraged when one husband decided to forgive his unfaithful wife that he had the man's name removed from the list of those eligible for jury duty.

Not that his own life would stand too much scrutiny from the point of view of personal morality. Domitian's affairs with his various mistresses went on. But if Domitia was an admirably understanding wife, Domitian was a deeply jealous husband. When, in 83 C.E., he heard that Domitia was having an affair with Paris, a celebrated Egyptian actor, he had him murdered in the street, while Domitia was divorced and exiled.

The vengeful Emperor reacted with fury when he saw the spontaneous outburst of mass mourning for Paris, considered a great star by the people. Outraged to hear that fans of Paris had been making a sort of shrine of the place where he had been murdered, Domitian had several individuals executed for placing flowers and perfume there. He even had one of Paris' students put to death because of a fancied resemblance to his late teacher.

This episode is all too typical of Domitian's reign. With all the powers at his disposal, he was desperately thin-skinned. He went into a demented rage at

THE VESTAL VIRGINS

Rome's famous 'Vestal Virgins' were the priests of Vesta, goddess of the hearth. They tended the sacred fire that was kept eternally alight in Vesta's temple beside the Forum. That fire represented the everlasting warmth of the Roman home. The chastity of the Vestal Virgins symbolized the eternal fidelity of Roman womanhood and the perpetual security of the Roman state.

Any fall from grace by a Vestal Virgin was therefore taken very seriously, and the punishment was extremely severe. At the same time, though, these women were so sacred that the city was not supposed to take their lives.

Hence the horrible tradition by which a Vestal Virgin convicted of impurity was to be taken outside the city limits to the Campus Sceleratus or 'Wicked Field'. There she was walled up in an underground cell. She would be left with a few days' food and water. That way, the reasoning

went, because she was alive when she entered the room and had been given means of sustenance, then it couldn't be said that the Romans were killing her.

In practice, this punishment was very seldom carried out, and most known examples date from the early days of the Republic. Even in 84 C.E., when three Vestal Virgins were convicted of impurity, they were executed in the usual way, by strangulation. In 90 C.E., though, when Cornelia, chief of the Vestal Virgins, broke her vows, Domitian had her pay the traditional penalty. The men with whom she had sinned were beaten to death with wooden rods.

The Vestal Virgins were the keepers of the flame, tending the fire kept burning everlastingly in the Temple of Vesta, goddess of the hearth. The Virgins and their untouched purity symbolized the grace and chastity of Roman womanhood.

Two pools and a line of statues are now all that remains of the House of the Vestal Virgins in Rome. This open atrium was the heart of a massive, three-storey residence grand enough to accommodate the women who represented the eternal honour of the city.

Roman emperors were touchy: paranoia went with the territory and they came down on hard on any sign of sedition. Whether the threat came from political rivals, irreverent satirists or Christian saints (here we see St John the Evangelist narrowly escaping death by boiling oil), the response was likely to be violent and swift.

anything that might conceivably be interpreted as a slight. Hence he cracked down on the traditional custom of circulating smutty satires about public figures. Once, at a gladiatorial show, he overheard a man making some irreverent witticism at his expense. He had him pulled from his place in the crowd and thrown into the arena to be torn apart by savage dogs.

POLITICAL PARANOIA

Senators who were guilty of ill-considered quips also found themselves in the deepest possible trouble. Aelius Lamia, Domitia's former husband, who had been forced to divorce her against his will, made a mildly wry remark about it some years later. He paid for this with his life. The jokes didn't even have to be at Domitian's expense. Another senator, Mettius Pompusianus, offended the Emperor's sense of patriotic propriety by naming two of his slaves Hannibal and Mago. Rome had, of course, successfully seen off both these Carthaginian generals and razed their city to the ground in 146 B.C.E., so it is hard to see how this facetiousness was really hurting anybody. Domitian was implacable, though. One statesman, Salvius Cocceianus, was put to death for celebrating the birthday of the late Emperor Otho, who happened to be his paternal uncle.

Such absurdities may easily mask the seriousness of Domitian's reign of terror, because he displayed a more deep-seated paranoia. He was more than a match for any of the Caesars when it came to seeing

THE BLACK BANQUET

Domitian made a point of being a generous Emperor, much to the detriment of the imperial treasury. He was forever treating the populace to spectacles and shows. His nobles, though, he entertained in a rather more sinister way when he invited them to a macabre 'black banquet' at his palace.

He had prepared for the event by having his banqueting chamber painted entirely black – its walls, its ceiling, its floor and furniture. His guests were warned to come alone, without any of their womenfolk or their attendants. On arrival, they were ushered into this grim and gloomy room.

It got worse. Naked boys, painted black from head to foot, pranced in like demons, carrying black boards made to look like grave-markers. Each board was inscribed with the name of a guest, and it was set up solemnly beside the couch where that man was placed. The food that was brought was of the sort sanctified by tradition for offering at the graves of the dead. The dishes in which they were served were black, of course.

Thoroughly spooked, the guests sat there and listened in terror as Domitian discoursed cheerfully of death and slaughter for several hours. Eventually, the Emperor suggested that it was time for them to go home. They felt a thrill of relief, until it became clear that they were going to be taken, singly and separately in litters, by the Emperor's slaves rather than their own.

They were transfixed by the certainty that they would 'disappear' en route after leaving the imperial palace, and that their bodies would be found in some out-of-the-way alley next day, or never found at all. By the time they did get home, perfectly safely, their nerves were in shreds. They collapsed in their relief as they went in through their doors.

And then, just minutes later, a messenger from the Emperor suddenly arrived. They felt this was finally it. They were really going to die. Instead each was given his grave-marker redone in silver, along with the dishes he had been served at supper, but this time in vessels of the costliest materials.

All's well that ends well, maybe, but Rome's patricians somehow never felt these lavish gifts could even begin to offset the terror their host had forced them to endure that evening.

TORTURE AND TRUTH

Today, if torture is frowned upon, it is not only on humanitarian grounds, but also because we distrust the kind of information it supplies. Under extreme duress, a suspect is likely to blurt out whatever he or she thinks the torturer wants to hear, just to bring the ordeal to an end.

In ancient times, however, it wasn't looked at that way. Torture was seen as the only guarantee of truth. Only in agonizing pain, it was assumed, would the instinct to lie be bypassed, allowing the interrogator to get to the real story. This was especially the case with slaves, thought to be naturally sleazy and dishonest. Slaves' evidence was only accepted in courts if it had been obtained by torture. Many Roman patricians convicted of crimes were found guilty on the evidence of household slaves 'persuaded' to inform against their masters.

subversion wherever he looked, and his persecutions cut a swathe through the senatorial class. He had 20 of Rome's leading patricians killed, at the very least. And then there was the sheer cruelty of the way Domitian's henchmen went to work, beating and torturing in their efforts to uncover the conspiracies he thought were

---

One statesman, Salvius Cocceianus, was put to death for celebrating the birthday of the late Emperor Otho, who happened to be his paternal uncle.

---

lurking everywhere. Hundreds were snatched from the streets and from their homes, flung into cells and forced to tell the Emperor's interrogators what they wanted to know. It was on Domitian's own orders that fire was applied to their genitals, an innovation in the Roman torture manual.

Domitian enjoyed the sufferings of others, and he liked to play little power games. He was never more charming to the consul Arrecinus Clemens than in the days before he had him killed for alleged conspiracy. And when he had decided to kill one of his stewards, he had the man sit beside him on his couch and share his meal one evening, paying him every affectionate attention. He sent him away happy and buoyant, before having him crucified the next day. When suspects were convicted at his trials, he would tease them by hinting that he was seriously thinking of showing clemency, before, as ever, condemning them to death.

A CLOSE RELATIONSHIP

That Domitian had a more tender side is clear from his attachment to Julia Flavia. She was Titus' daughter by his second marriage and so Domitian's niece. She was closer to him in age than might be assumed, being

only 13 years his junior, but then she was far too close for comfort in terms of kinship. No matter. The Emperor seduced her when she was still married, to the consul Titus Flavius Sabinus. Like Domitia's husband before him, this unfortunate man was now hounded out of office and into the divorce court (he was afterwards executed), all so that the Emperor could have the woman he wanted.

They lived together as husband and wife for the best part of a decade, until Julia's sudden death in 91 C.E. It was said in Rome that she had been pregnant by the Emperor, who had forced her into having an abortion. She had then died when the procedure went badly wrong. However brutal the Emperor had been in determining that their baby would not be born, he was overcome with grief at Julia's loss and had her deified.

Her death was the cue for Domitian to decide to forgive and forget where Domitia was concerned. She was brought back from her exile and reunited with her former husband. They remained together from that time on, although they never actually remarried.

> Hundreds were ... forced to tell the Emperor's interrogators what they wanted to know. It was on Domitian's orders that fire was applied to their genitals, an innovation in the torture manual.

In his eagerness to interfere in the running of the Empire when he first came to the throne, Domitian had actually righted many wrongs. Where he found the justice system had unfairly punished someone, he often strove to rectify the situation. He reinstated officials

BOX: DOMITIAN AND THE DIRT

At the start of Domitian's reign, the Talmud tells us, the famous Rabbi Akiva ben Joseph led a deputation to Rome. They took with them a gift for the new Emperor in the form of a box containing some of the sacred earth of the Promised Land. Unfortunately, it looked as though they were fated never to reach their destination. A violent storm blew up and threatened to swamp their ship.

The rabbi raised his arms and prayed, however, and within moments the waves were still. All on board were astonished at the miracle he had worked. Among them was Titus Flavius Clemens, a highly born Roman and close relative of the Emperor. He offered to put in a good word for Akiva's delegation when they got to Rome.

In the event, he had to use all the persuasive powers he could muster. The over-sensitive Domitian reacted with fury to his gift. To him it seemed no more than a heap of dirt, and he

Clemens by name and clement by nature, Titus Flavius Clemens, a high-born Roman, was a good friend to the Jewish people – and ultimately a convert.

immediately decided that it was an intentional insult. He sentenced the Jewish visitors to death. Fortunately, though, before they could be executed, Clemens had succeeded in calming the Emperor down.

Already impressed by Akiva after his experiences on the ship, Clemens found him more and more inspiring as he got to know him in the course of his negotiations. Eventually, Clemens decided to convert to Judaism himself and became a friend of the Jewish people in the capital.

As Domitian's reign went on, Rome became a far more uncomfortable place for the Jews. The Emperor eventually denounced Clemens as a traitor to Roman religion, and he was condemned to death. Before his execution, though, he is said to have circumcised himself and adopted the new name Shalom Ketiah. His widow, Flavia Domitilla, was actually Domitian's niece, the daughter of his beloved elder sister. This is the reason, perhaps, for her escape from the episode alive. She was exiled to Pandateria and eventually ended up both revered in Jewish tradition and a Christian saint.

who had been improperly dismissed and restored property that had been unjustly confiscated. But his good intentions were soon overwhelmed by the growing scale of the crisis brought on by his tinkering in the economy at large.

With the Empire facing bankruptcy, he decided he would raise money any way he could, and as Emperor his powers were pretty well limitless. Domitian's paranoia is well documented, but soon it was surpassed by his hunger for revenue. Political suspicion became just an excuse for seizures of property on a colossal scale. A word out of turn, a suggestion of disloyalty passed on by some stranger, at second- or third-hand – any such thing was enough to damn an individual in the Emperor's eyes. After all, the reality was that treason was no longer the issue. If a person possessed wealth, Domitian wanted it, so the 'traitors' were still put to death. Of course, only when they had been convicted and killed did their property pass to Domitian and the state.

Domitian was fanatically alert. He was particularly anxious in the middle of the day, because an astrologer had once predicted that he would die at that time.

It was for financial reasons, rather than what we would now regard as 'racist' prejudice, that Domitian went to war with the Jews of Rome. Titus had imposed a tax on the Jews in return for the right to practise their religion, but he hadn't really bothered to enforce it. Domitian was far more energetic in exacting this tax than his brother had been. And he was unrelenting in his attempts to track down those he thought were avoiding it. He became convinced that his capital was full of non-declared Jews, worshipping secretly to escape their payments to the state. Suspects were summoned to public hearings, where they were examined for signs of circumcision. At the slightest suggestion of sharp practice, their property was confiscated altogether.

IMPERIAL ENDGAME

As his reign wore on, and he made himself more and more enemies, Domitian's paranoia became more personal and more intense. He felt haunted by fear every hour of the day. He had the cloisters where he walked refaced with a shiny, polished stone so that it would reflect a would-be assassin approaching from behind.

Like Claudius and Caligula before him, though, his fears became self-fulfilling. His enemies knew that, whatever they did, the Emperor would bring about their destruction, so they felt they had no alternative but to work to bring about his. Many plots were discovered – some imaginary, some real – but in the end, in 96 C.E., one was successfully followed through.

It was a far-reaching conspiracy, involving not only members of the Senate but palace staff and even Domitia, the unofficial Empress. She appears to have felt that her position was insecure and she did not want to be sent away a second time. Stephanus was the man appointed to strike the blow. He was steward to Flavia Domitilla, the Emperor's other niece, his late sister's daughter. But he had fallen under suspicion more recently because Domitian thought he had been stealing household funds. So, Stephanus knew his days were numbered, and that he had nothing to lose now by acting, and he was happy to undertake the assassination.

NOT THE TIME TO DIE

Wrapping his wrist in a thick cloth, claiming that he had injured his hand in a household accident, he used this as concealment for a dagger. In the event, he had to dog the Emperor's steps for several days while he waited for an opportunity to strike. In his paranoia, Domitian was fanatically alert. He was particularly anxious in the middle of the day, because an astrologer had once predicted that he would die at that time. On the day he was finally murdered, the conspirators soothed those anxieties by getting his boy attendant to tell his master that the hour was far later than it really was.

Reassured, the Emperor relaxed his vigilance and sat down to get on with some official business. Stephanus walked quickly up behind him and stabbed him. His fellow conspirators then streamed into the chamber and joined in the attack. Domitian had at least seven further wounds when he at last lay dead.

With his laurel wreath and his air of command, Domitian makes a convincing emperor in this Renaissance Italian painting, but his reign was mostly marred by a paranoia born of inadequacy.

DOMITIANVS·AVG

VI

GOOD MEN ... MOSTLY

Politically, economically and psychologically, the Empire would scarcely have survived another reign like Domitian's, so it was fortunate that the following period brought a breathing-space. The 'Five Good Emperors' weren't perfect, but they were a vast improvement on what had gone before.

✦

Domitian's body was still warm when the Senate swung into action and named his successor. Marcus Cocceius Nerva was the man they chose. He was already 66 but that was very much a good thing. The senators never intended him as anything more than a caretaker-ruler. It helped too that he didn't have a child. In 123 years of imperial rule, Rome had already experienced two dynasties, and it wasn't in a hurry to see another taking power. Not content with dominating the Senate and the patrician

class, Domitian had sometimes seemed set on destroying it. Rome's nobility wanted someone in charge who was a little calmer and more cooperative.

They certainly got it in Nerva. He was to go down in history as the first of the 'Five Good Emperors', under whom the Empire was generally peaceful and well governed. Nerva's first act as Emperor was to announce that no senators would go to their deaths as long as he was on the throne. The terror of the Domitian years was over. To underline that message, the Senate promptly declared a *damnatio memoriae* ('damnation of the memory') on Domitian: his name was expunged from all official records; his coins melted down; his statues smashed; his inscriptions erased. If only his memory really could have been wiped away so easily. Rome was still a society in shock.

Nerva's accession came as a welcome relief after the state-sponsored terror of Domitian's reign: he acted swiftly to restore a state of calm. He was the first of five 'Good Emperors', of whom Hadrian (above) was the third: they presided over something of a golden age.

Nerva worked as hard as he could to undo the damage. He took steps to restore property unjustly confiscated by his predecessor. This represented quite a cost for the economy, but the new administration went a surprisingly long way to making up the shortfall simply by melting down Domitian's gold and silver statues. Nerva was taking more risks when he announced that there would be no new public building projects and, especially, that he would not be staging any games or shows. Rome might not have been a democracy, but its populace had certain privileges sanctioned by tradition, and chief among them was the right to be entertained with lavish spectacles. Rather than hailing Nerva's vision and welcoming his good housekeeping, the people thought he was a mean-spirited party pooper.

PRAETORIAN PRISONER

Also unhappy was the army. Its enthusiastic support had effectively been bought by Domitian's generosity over the years. So lavish had Domitian been, indeed, that the legions had wanted Domitian deified at his death. The Praetorian Guard had been treated especially well by the late Emperor. They had taken it very badly when he was killed, and still worse when one of the conspirators was appointed their new Prefect.

> The Praetorian Guard had made it very clear that it could topple Nerva any time it wanted to and that from then on its members would be watching his every move.

Fearing a mutiny, Nerva was forced to reinstate Domitian's commander, Casperius Aelianus. Not that this was to restore the Guard's loyalty in the longer term. On the contrary, in 97 C.E., Aelianus led his men in a military uprising against Nerva. They marched on the imperial palace and took him prisoner. Those they held responsible for Domitian's assassination had still not been brought to justice, and they remained in their positions at the court. The mutineers were determined that they should be held to account for their actions. They rooted them out and executed them there and then.

TRAJAN TRANSFER

The action could not really be called a coup, because Nerva was neither hurt nor explicitly overthrown, but his authority was hardly enhanced by these events. The Praetorian Guard had made it very clear that it could topple him any time it wanted to and that from then on its members would be watching his every move. In hopes of appeasing them, Nerva started casting around for a successor who he thought likely to be acceptable to the military.

He would always have had to make a ruling on who was to come after him as Emperor. Childless as he was, he was going to leave a dangerous power vacuum if he didn't. Suddenly, in 97 C.E., when he was in his sixties, he became a father of sorts by announcing his adoption of Marcus Ulpius Traianus. Trajan, as he is now generally known, was himself a strange age to become a son. He had been born in Italica, near Seville, Spain, in 53 C.E. That made him aged 44 at the time of his adoption, and he had already won great distinction as a general, which was his great recommendation as Nerva's new 'son', of course.

Though the Ulpius clan was a distinguished one and his father had been Governor of Syria in the mid-70s C.E., Trajan was seen as having made his own way in life. A career soldier who had joined up at an early age, he was definitely regarded as one of the army's own. He had served in some of the toughest campaigns of the age and was making a mark for himself on the German frontier when the news of his adoption was announced.

He came back to Rome, where Nerva gave him the rank of consul and set him up by his side as his co-ruler. But in the weeks and months that followed, Nerva fairly quickly disengaged and allowed his 'son' and successor-designate to take charge. When the elderly Emperor died at the end of January 98 C.E., and Trajan formally ascended the throne, it really didn't make much difference. The new ruler had already been in power for some time.

Adopted at the age of 44, Trajan did his new 'father' Nerva proud, and made him the perfect successor on his death. The Roman Empire reached its largest extent during Trajan's reign.

THE FIVE GOOD EMPERORS

After Domitian, anyone would have been an improvement, but there is no doubt that Nerva was a good man. More than that, he had shown himself a wise and effective ruler under pressure. His reign ushered in an extended period of more or less enlightened and successful rule, which would see the Empire happily and prosperously through to the latter part of the second century. Nerva's successor Trajan gave way to Hadrian, who was followed by Antoninus Pius. Marcus Aurelius then reigned until 180 C.E.

RESPECT THROUGH VIRTUE
Ironically, the 'Five Good Emperors' designation originated with the Renaissance political theorist Niccolò Macchiavelli, now mostly famous for his manual of no-holds-barred political cynicism, *The Prince*. In that book, the 'good' ruler is the one who knows how to win power and then hold onto it, whatever ruthlessness or unscrupulousness that may take. Macchiavelli seems to have meant it more conventionally, though, in writing of

Hadrian (right) was the third of the 'Five Good Emperors', and ruled the Empire with a firm hand.

the Five Good Emperors. All these rulers, he says, managed to do without violent bodyguards and military might, earning their protection through their virtue and the people's love for them.

Nerva must have felt that his adoption of Trajan had been thrust upon him, and the two men had little obviously in common. But when the 'son' succeeded his 'father', he seemed a chip off the old block. There was a clear 'family resemblance' in the way he ruled. Trajan continued Nerva's work of trying to undo the damage done by Domitian. He freed prisoners, called home exiles and made restitution to those who had been unjustly dispossessed.

THE BEST OF EMPERORS
So well was he regarded that the Senate voted him an official title of *Optimus* ('the Best'), and his taste for booze and boys was indulgently overlooked. Some did tut-tut that Trajan was too easy in his treatment of Abgarus of Edessa, king of the Mesopotamian kingdom of Osroene, because he fancied his famously good-looking son, Arbandes, but few felt inclined to hold such foibles against him. For not only was Trajan just and effective in his domestic policy, but also he

Completed in 113 C.E., and standing just under 30m (100ft) tall, Trajan's Column is a monument worthy of one of the greatest generals of the Roman Empire. Spiralling around it, like a sort of epic cartoon strip, runs a carved relief representing the events of the commander's victorious campaign in Dacia.

was extremely successful in the military field abroad. He won a series of brilliant victories in the Dacian Wars, beyond the Danube in what is now Romania and Moldova. Back in Rome, after a magnificent triumph, a spectacular column was erected out of admiration for him. Finished in 113 C.E., it was made of marble and carved in a spiral with detailed scenes from his campaign. Trajan also conquered territories in the Middle East, in what are now Jordan and northwestern Saudi Arabia, as well as in Armenia and Mesopotamia (modern Iraq). On his campaign he took Hadrian, the son of his late cousin, with him, whom he had taken into his care as a young orphan.

It was under Trajan that the Empire grew to its fullest extent, stretching from Scotland to the shores of the Caspian Sea. And Trajan would have added fresh conquests had he not, toward the end of 116 C.E., suddenly been taken ill. He was forced to set out on the long and arduous homeward journey back to Rome. In the event, he was not destined to make it there. On 9 August 117 C.E., having adopted Hadrian as his son and successor, he died in Selinus, a former Greek colony in Armenia.

THE LAST ACT

Or did he? The events of Trajan's final days are surrounded by confusion and conspiracy, with speculation around Pompeia Plotina, the Emperor's wife. Not, for a change, because it was suspected that she had anything to do with his death. Theirs appears to have been a genuinely happy marriage, and she was a woman of intelligence and decency. She was renowned for her studies in the Greek

Pompeia Plotina, Trajan's wife, was held in the highest respect for her virtue and abilities: she could take much of the credit for the achievements of her husband's reign. Devoted as she was to their adopted son Hadrian, she schemed benignly to ease him into the succession.

philosophers and held to have been a deeply positive influence on her husband's rule, advancing the interests of the poor and outsiders in society.

Plotina was no Messalina then, nor an Agrippina the Younger. She was, however, a childless woman

---

> It was under Trajan that the Empire grew to its fullest extent, stretching from Scotland to the shores of the Caspian Sea.

---

who had grown attached to the ward she had helped bring up from boyhood. Although Hadrian's place in Trajan's affections was secure, Plotina had been eager for her husband to adopt him formally, and this is where her motives have been called into question.

When Trajan died, the whisperers said, he had still not got round to an adoption ceremony (he had been on campaign for years, and lately he had been sick). When he died, therefore, Plotina paid an actor to impersonate her husband and maintain the fiction that he was still alive. It was this impostor who, as 'Trajan', acknowledged Hadrian as his own and named him as his heir to the Empire. Whether this story is true or not, it is evident that Hadrian owed a great deal to Plotina, and no surprise that one of his first actions as Emperor was to have her deified.

A BAD START

In Rome, there were mutterings about the paperwork relating to Hadrian's adoption as Trajan's son, but by this time it hardly mattered any more. Hadrian had the army on his side. He had seen off a bid for the throne by Lusius Quietus, and he had the support of Publius Acilius Attianus. Trajan's

THE NEARLY MAN

Lusius Quietus, who very nearly beat Hadrian to the throne in 117 C.E., is a fascinating figure in his own right. He came from a North African Moorish background. His father was a Berber tribal chief who had allied himself with the Romans in Claudius' time. Lusius himself had risen to great prominence in the Empire. The Romans were utterly intolerant towards cultures they regarded as alien, believing that all their subjects should fit in with their way of doing things. However, the Romans don't seem to have worried too much about what we would nowadays call 'race'.

Lusius Quietus actually succeeded in keeping some of his own tribal traditions alive in a military career that brought him considerable distinction as a cavalry commander. Historically, he was in the right place at the right time for this. The Dacian and Parthian campaigns had brought Rome up against the mounted warriors of the western steppe, and his desert horsemen had been able to offer an important counter.

He was just the sort of heroic stuff that a successful Emperor might be made of, then, and when Trajan died Lusius moved swiftly to seize power. Not as swiftly as Hadrian, though. He was on the spot in Selinus and was immediately acclaimed as Emperor. Seeing the threat from Lusius, Hadrian gave an imperial order for his cavalry to be disbanded, but his loyal warriors refused to comply with this command. Armed force was sent against them, and still they wouldn't surrender. In the end, they fought to the death to defend their lord. Hadrian finally prevailed, though, and had Lusius executed. The most formidable threat to his authority was gone.

As this scene from Trajan's Column reminds us, the Dacian Wars pitted the power of Rome against the mounted warriors of the steppe. Here it was that Lusius Quietus had come into his own, with his Berber background, and his skills in the arts of cavalry warfare.

sometime Prefect had in fact been Hadrian's co-guardian and he remained loyal to his ward as Emperor. He did not waste time either, but, identifying those in the Senate who, he thought, might be hostile to Hadrian's accession, Attianus had them all arrested and put to death. He had, he claimed, uncovered an assassination plot against the Emperor. In truth, however, the only murderer here was Attianus.

It was fortunate for Hadrian that all this happened when he was still straightening out the affairs of the Empire in the east, so he wasn't directly implicated in the actions of his Prefect. In fairness, no one seems to have been more conscious than Hadrian himself of how unpromising a start this cynical bloodletting was to his reign. He quickly relieved Attianus of his duties and made him retire from public life.

Hadrian then set about the business of ruling. He saw himself as a consolidator rather than a conqueror. It was at his initiative that Rome started establishing a fixed frontier at this time. Constructions such as Hadrian's Wall in the north of England, and similar fortifications in Germany and along the Danube, amounted to a declaration that the Roman Empire was officially big enough. The task of its rulers from now on would not be the addition of fresh provinces, but to defend those territories it had already, to maintain the *Pax Romana* ('Roman Peace').

THE JEWISH PROBLEM

Titus and his generals had dealt Jewish dreams of independence a shattering blow in their brutal campaigns of the 70s C.E., but the spirit of rebellion had not died at Masada. A second rebellion of 115–17 C.E., subsequently known as the 'Kitos War', had rocked the Empire during Trajan's reign. Roman commentators accused the insurgents of terrible atrocities: of sawing living soldiers in half; of mutilation, even cannibalism; of more than half a million innocent settlers savagely murdered. Lusius Quietus had been equally ruthless in his response.

These hostilities had only just come to a bloody end when Hadrian ascended the imperial throne, and

he later made a point of paying a visit to Judaea. Not just that, but he gave every appearance of being conciliatory, even generous, in his attitude. He undertook to rebuild the city of Jerusalem, which had once more been razed in the recent fighting. He would rebuild the Temple too, he promised the grateful Jews.

> Hadrian had no intention of rebuilding the old Jerusalem. Why would anyone want to reconstruct that anarchic confusion of winding lanes and narrow alleys? Instead he would treat the Jews to a sparkling new city in the Roman style ...

He wasn't lying, exactly, but it quickly became clear how great a gulf of misunderstanding lay between the new Emperor and his Jewish subjects. A firm believer in the Roman way of doing things, Hadrian had no intention of rebuilding the old Jerusalem. Why would anyone want to reconstruct that old anarchic confusion of winding lanes and narrow alleys? Instead he would treat the Jews to a sparkling new city in the Roman style, with a noble forum, and spacious streets on a rational, grid-like plan. It was actually a point of pride with the Romans that they had built substantially the same urban conurbations over and over again from North Africa to Britain and from Spain to Syria.

This was never going to satisfy the Jews, a people passionately attached to their cultural traditions. Still less did they like the Emperor's plans for their ancient Temple. Sure, it was going to be rebuilt, but it was going to be dedicated, not to Yahweh, their sole, all-powerful deity, but to Jupiter, father of the Roman gods. In short, Hadrian was determined to drag the Jews out of their benighted religious observances and 'civilize' them into following those of Rome.

A MESSIAH MAKES TROUBLE

In 131 C.E., regardless of Jewish opposition, Hadrian had work on the Temple site commence. An extra legion was sent to Judaea to ensure order. The

Running for 120km (75 miles) across the narrow neck of northern Britain, Hadrian's Wall was at once a proclamation of Roman might and an admission of its limits. Hadrian established similar 'fixed frontiers' in other places around the edge of the Empire.

Romans' inauguration ceremony started with the ritual breaking of the ground, itself an act of sacrilege in Jewish law. Unperturbed, the Emperor decided that this was a good moment to prohibit the practice of circumcision, which was, in his opinion, no more than a mark of barbarism.

A volatile situation was ignited by the appearance on the scene of Simon Bar Kokhba, whose followers

> Hadrian decided that this was a good moment to prohibit the practice of circumcision, which was, in his opinion, no more than a mark of barbarism.

claimed that he was the Messiah. This great king, predicted by the prophets, was to be sent by God to deliver the Jews from their subjection and to usher in an age of peace on earth. Simon's messianic movement found a champion in Domitian's old adversary the Rabbi Akiva, who said that Simon was the one prophesied by the biblical Book of Numbers. 'A star shall rise out of Jacob,' we read there in Chapter 24, verse 17; 'and a sceptre shall spring up in Israel.' Since Simon's name 'Bar Kokhba' was the Aramaic for 'son of a star', it was clear that he was the ruler whose coming had been promised.

JERUSALEM CAPTURED

This vision of the coming of God's kingdom on the earth of Israel clearly didn't conform with the Roman's strategy for Judaea, but Simon's supporters succeeded in keeping their plans for rebellion under wraps. In 132 C.E., they made their move, catching the Roman garrison in Jerusalem unawares and quickly taking control of the capital.

Hadrian was enraged, but also badly disconcerted because the Romans really had not seen this rebellion coming. With his armies busy dealing with local

Jewish anger had been smouldering since the time of Titus; Hadrian's heavy-handed policies provoked a fresh eruption. Caught completely unawares, the Emperor lost the initiative and the rebels prevailed for a time: it took the most monstrous bloodletting to re-establish Roman control.

unrest along the northern frontiers, there really wasn't very much that he could do. For now, at least, Hadrian could only stand by while the rebels had the run of Jerusalem. They established an independent Jewish state under the spiritual leadership of Rabbi Akiva, who proclaimed the 'Era of the Redemption of Israel'.

PAYING THE PRICE

In the end, the Jews paid heavily for humiliating the might of Rome. A seasoned general, Sextus Julius Severus, was summoned back from Britain and placed at the head of an enormous army. It headed south in 133 C.E., marching on Judaea in overwhelming force. And it was in a grimly determined mood. There were to be no more revolts. They army were going to sort out the Jewish problem once and for all.

For the Jews, whose uprising had been inspired by the messianic Simon Bar Kokhba (above), among others, it was the utterly unthinkable. For the legionaries it was just another day at work. In 133 C.E., Roman troops violated the sanctity of the Temple. In truth, it never occurred to Hadrian that he wasn't doing the Jews a great favour: Roman ways were self-evidently superior.

Antinous was the surpassing love of Hadrian's life: his death in 130 C.E. left the Emperor desolate. Of course, his tragic demise had one real advantage in what was very much an idealizing passion: the beauty never had to fade or the youth grow old.

They did so in no uncertain terms. The Talmud estimates the number of Jewish deaths in millions, but it then goes on to say that the Roman horses were up to their bridles in blood, so it seems likely that there was a degree of exaggeration. Yet even Roman historians give a Jewish death toll of well over half a million. (Not that Roman casualties were negligible, by any means. The Jews resisted to the death, and one Roman legion was entirely wiped out.) Almost a thousand villages were destroyed, their populations massacred as a scorched-earth policy was pursued to prevent regrouping and recovery. In addition, fifty rebel fortresses were flattened to prevent any possibility of a further rebellion in the future.

JERUSALEM RENAMED
In truth, it didn't appear that Judaea was going to have much of a future. Hadrian redoubled his efforts to stamp out Jewish religious practice. Sacred scrolls were burned, rabbis executed and the Torah (the Jewish law) was banned. The Temple was turned over to the worship of Jupiter, and of Hadrian himself. To add insult to injury, Jerusalem was renamed *Aelia Capitolina,* while Judaea became *Palestinae.* As for the Jews themselves, they weren't quite eliminated, and their creed quietly continued 'underground' in the outlying settlements. But hundreds of thousands had been killed, and many of the survivors were sold into slavery or forced to flee into exile. Some scholars argue that the long centuries of exile in the 'diaspora' started here.

A BEAUTIFUL BOY
But the Judaean campaign stood out in what was for the most part a peaceful reign. Hadrian, by and large, preferred to make love not war. And the love of his life was Antinous, a youth he is believed to have encountered when he was journeying in Bithynia around 124 C.E. At that time, Antinous was about 14, and Hadrian himself in his late forties. The Greeks had settled Bithynia, in northwestern Turkey, in centuries gone by, and Antinous himself was of Greek parentage. Hadrian had long been an ardent fan of all things

Greek. In fact, as a youth he had been nicknamed *Graeculus* ('little Greek'). He was a devotee of Greek poetry, history and philosophy. But, it seemed, most of all he loved 'Greek love'.

It was not, of course, unusual for Roman men to have sexual relations with youths and boys, and no stigma was attached to those who did. But these rough-and-ready couplings were not generally regarded with any great seriousness – just seen matter-of-factly as something the red-blooded male naturally did. It certainly wasn't regarded as representing a separate sexuality that might preclude marriage or sex with female concubines. Hadrian, however, had bought into the Classical Greek romance of pederasty, in which the love between man and youth was idealized as the love between experience and unspoiled perfection. He celebrated his love for Antinous, advertising and romanticizing it, and making it his reason for living in what was seen as a most un-Roman way.

> Hadrian had bought into the Classical Greek romance of pederasty, in which the love between man and youth was idealized as the love between experience and unspoiled perfection.

Hadrian was married. His wife was his third cousin, Vibia Sabina. Their relationship never seems to have been a happy one, and certainly produced no children. Sabina was said to have had an affair with one of her husband's slaves. In the absence of any testimony about affairs with women on Hadrian's part, it doesn't seem too big a reach to conclude that he simply wasn't interested in heterosexual sex.

CONSTANT COMPANION
Although he may have been no more than a page at first, Antinous was soon the Emperor's constant companion. He accompanied him on all his travels around the Empire. They were inseparable for six years, until in 130 C.E., on a visit to Egypt, Antinous drowned in the Nile River. No one knew how, or why,

Hadrian lost no time in having his favourite deified. Shrines were established across the Empire, as here at Leptis Magna, Libya. Antinous' cult encouraged an aesthetic emphasis which had until now been understated in Roman culture, a reverence for grace and beauty for their own sakes.

it had happened. Speculation has continued to this day as to whether it was purely an accident, or murder, suicide or some sort of sacrificial ritual.

Hadrian was heartbroken. He was never to get over Antinous' loss. He gave orders for his deification. The cult of Antinous the god actually caught on in a major way, and statues of the beautiful youth have been found far and wide at sites across the Empire. Its main focus, appropriately enough, included Antinous' birthplace, Bithynia, and Athens, the Classical capital of 'Greek love'. There was an important shrine, too, at Antinopolis, the city Hadrian had founded on the banks of the Nile near the place where his young lover had met his death. Antinous also had a place in the heavens. Hadrian had a cluster of stars named after him, although the name fell out of use when astronomers reclassified the constellations in 1930.

That Hadrian had been to Judaea at the start of his reign, that he had found Antinous in Bithynia and that he had lost him in Egypt seems unremarkable enough from our point of view. To the Romans, though, the extent of Hadrian's travels seemed extraordinary,

'GREEK LOVE'

Homosexuality has had a part to play in many of the world's great warrior cultures. Older men would have relations with young recruits as part of their initiation into the corps and the recruits' induction into its code of martial values.

That seems to be how it came to be a part of Classical Greek culture, and it is clearly present in the heroic tradition described by Homer. Over time, though, it came to transcend the military sphere. The older man had a role to play in educating the youth, morally and intellectually, equipping him to take his place as an adult in society. The sexual relationship between them was seen as central to this process. Only in the intensity of the adolescent's love for his mentor would his feeling for his society take shape. Meanwhile, the man's love for his protégé showed his love for the perfection he represented in the form of his beauty and his moral innocence.

Greek philosophers such as Socrates, Plato and Aristotle wrote inspirationally of the love between teacher and student, but they abstained from writing about the messy realities of its physical

Greek 'humanism' involved a new appreciation of the possibilities for artistic and scientific endeavour. At its heart was an exalted delight in the beauty of the male form.

expression. Plato, in particular, wrote in praise of a pure, physically chaste and rarefied intellectual passion, hence the modern term 'Platonic love'.

THE EMPIRE IN MINIATURE

Hadrian found Rome wearying, which was one reason why he stayed away so much. In latter years, though, and without Antinous, he could not face it at all. He fled the capital whenever he possibly could and was never happier than he was getting away from it all at his rural residence near Tivoli. He had built it himself, and it was called the Villa Adriana – although the word 'villa' barely begins to describe this astonishing 100-hectare (250-acre) complex. Its more than 30 buildings included multiple palaces, libraries, baths and temples. Much of the site has still not been excavated, but what has been uncovered is almost beyond belief.

The Villa Adriana was Hadrian's rural retreat: here he lived his idea of the simple life, although it was a 'simple life' of the utmost splendour. In its architecture and layout, the complex expressed his personality, his passions: for beauty, for learning, for travel – and for Antinous' memory.

The Emperor even had his own retreat-within-a-retreat. Behind a stately colonnade was a circular pond, and in the middle of that a tiny house upon an island. Hadrian would come here when he wanted complete seclusion. He could even have a drawbridge pulled up to keep the world at bay.

Hadrian had gone to ingenious lengths to preserve the serenity of the place. Hustle and bustle were banished behind the scenes. Slaves moved about the site, and shifted supplies, travelling through underground tunnels. There was a considerable network of these, some big enough to be negotiated by a horse and wagon.

> There were fountains, pools, shady grottoes and hidden nooks to be explored, and lovely statues to be admired.

But the most remarkable feature of the Villa Adriana was the way it crammed a world into one place. The Emperor had been a great journeyer in his time and was clearly eager to be reminded of his experiences. Different parts of the complex were named after different provinces of the Empire, with architecture and stylized scenery to match. Not surprisingly given Hadrian's enthusiasms, the predominating style was Greek. One feature of especially poignant interest was the Canopus, a long pool lined with columns and obelisks to suggest the Nile River. Here it was, of course, that Hadrian had lost his beloved Antinous, and this was his way of keeping love's memory alive.

Like the Gardens of Lucullus, the Villa Adriana's extensive grounds were meticulously landscaped. There were paths, walks, leafy groves and belvederes for the idler. There were fountains and pools, shady grottoes and hidden nooks to be explored, and lovely statues to be admired, many of them Greek antiques. The emphasis was on peace and quiet.

especially given that he didn't actually have to go. Certainly, the Romans were used to going away to war, otherwise they could never have conquered that vast empire. But while an Emperor might go on campaign and come back afterwards, that was pretty much it: no one stayed away from Rome for the sake of it.

Well, not quite no one. Nero had notoriously made a trip to Greece, although this had been taken as confirmation of his essential frivolity and the decadence of his reign. Hadrian, however, stayed on the move as a way of being a 'hands-on' emperor. At the same time, he obviously found the experience of travel a hugely rewarding one in its own right. So he became a 'working tourist'. He went to inspect the different provinces of the Empire, to praise good governors and chivy the slack, and he took lavish gifts wherever he went to keep local officials and clients sweet. He ordered public works, and often paid for them himself. He was given a particularly warm welcome in Nicomedia, in Bithynia, because he funded the reconstruction after a recent earthquake. He took a lively interest in every aspect of the economy, government and how the provinces defended themselves.

Leaving Rome in 121 C.E., Hadrian made his way through Gaul and crossed into Britain. 'Hadrian's Wall' was very much his brainchild. He oversaw the start of its construction in 122 C.E. before heading south to Hispania (Spain) and thence across the Straits of Gibraltar to Mauritania in North Africa. He then sailed east via Crete to the shores of modern Lebanon and pushed inland to Syria, before arcing northwest through Asia Minor (where he met Antinous), on through the Balkans and back to Italy. A few years later, though, he was off again. He went through Greece for another tour of Asia, in the course of which he made his unfortunate intervention in Judaea. If this ended badly for the Jews, his next stop, in Egypt, ended badly for him. It was here, of course, that he lost his beloved Antinous. After his love was gone, Hadrian seems to have lost his appetite for travel, perhaps even his appetite for life.

DUTIFUL SUCCESSORS
Throughout the 130s C.E., Hadrian's health declined. Ailing and in misery, he made a number of suicide attempts. Each time, however, his attendants managed to saved him. Given his efforts to commit suicide, though, it seems perverse that he should have reacted

angrily and launched a purge after a plot to assassinate him was uncovered. But there it was. Of the two young men he had adopted as his sons, meanwhile, one, named Lucius Aelius Caesar, died before Hadrian did himself. The other, Titus Aurelius Fulvius Boionius Arrius Antoninus, became his heir. Antoninus agreed, as a condition of his succession, that when he came to die himself he would ensure that Lucius Aelius Caesar's sons were first in line to the throne.

DUTIFUL AND EXEMPLARY EMPERORS
Hadrian died in 138 C.E. As Emperor, his successor became known as Antoninus Pius ('Antoninus the Dutiful') because of his efforts to have his adoptive father deified. He built him a splendid tomb, which was later to be adapted to use as a fortress, hence the name by which it is known today, Castel Sant'Angelo. Otherwise, Antoninus was too *pius* to have much to offer a book such as this. His reign was long and for the most part peaceful. He adored his wife Faustina and was devastated by her death in 141 C.E.; he had her deified and built her a temple in the Forum.

When Antoninus himself died, in his bed, 20 years later, Marcus Aurelius succeeded him. Antoninus had kept his promise in leaving the throne to Lucius Aelius Caesar's son. Marcus Aurelius was the last of the Five Good Emperors, a noted philosopher whose *Meditations* are still read widely today. He sealed his succession by marrying Antoninus' daughter, Faustina the Younger.

Marcus Aurelius was an exemplary leader, although his reign did see the beginnings of a looming threat to Rome. Far out in the eastern steppe, in Central Asia, a great movement of nomadic peoples was under way and pressure was building along the Empire's eastern frontier. For the moment, though, the problem appeared to be containable and the Empire proceeded prosperously on its way. In the end, Marcus Aurelius was to make only one real contribution to Rome's 'darker history', but that contribution was to be a big one. He named his son, Commodus, as his successor.

Marcus Aurelius dies a philosopher's death, undaunted by the prospect of eternity, as imagined by the French Romantic painter Eugène Délacroix. The last of the 'Good Emperors', Marcus Aurelius' one great mistake was to leave his throne to his son Commodus, a very bad emperor indeed.

VII

COMMODUS: AN EMPEROR UNHINGED

Of all the emperors, Commodus was the most utterly outrageous: hopelessly – often criminally – insane. Not content to reign over the Roman world, he wanted to reorder it, redefine its terms: the world was to be re-created with him as its centre.

◆

I t had been early in the eighth century that, in the wilds of the Tiber Valley, two orphan twins had been suckled by a she-wolf. The cave in which she was said to have nursed the boys was known as the Lupercal. Archeologists rediscovered it in 2007. Sadly, the inseparable brothers had eventually fought, and Romulus had killed his beloved Remus, but he had gone on to found the greatest city the world had ever seen.

Now that city was no more. After almost a thousand years of history, Rome had been abolished by imperial

Lucius Aurelius Commodus' portrait bust gave no hint of his extravagant obsessions. But then who would have thought that a son of the famous philosopher-emperor Marcus Aurelius would have turned out quite so strange – so far beyond eccentric as to be totally deranged?

decree. From now on, the urbanized area on the Tiber was to be known as *Colonia Lucia Annia Commodiana*, after its founder, the new Romulus, the Emperor Commodus. Lucius Aurelius Commodus had reigned alongside his father, Marcus Aurelius, from 177 C.E., becoming sole Emperor when he died in 180 C.E. Since then, Commodus had collected titles. In 182 C.E., he became *Pius* ('the Dutiful'). Three years later, he added *Felix*, ('the Fortunate', 'the Happy'). After that came *Invictus* ('Undefeated') and *Herculeus* ('Herculean'). By 192 C.E., when he was winding up the 'Eternal City' to found his own, all-new Commodian colony, he had accumulated no fewer than 12 titles. Enough, the thought seems to have struck him, to rename the months of the year in his own tribute. And this, to the confusion of all, he duly did.

In his mania to take personal possession of just about every aspect of life and civilization, he renamed the legions. They were no longer *legiones* but *commodianae*. The fleet that brought grain from North Africa to feed the people was now to be known as *Alexandria Commodiana Togata*, for all food, all nourishment, was to be seen as proceeding from Commodus. There were no Romans now, only *Commodiani*. From that time forth, every single citizen was to carry in his very identity the imprint of the great father, the founder, the all-providing Emperor.

COMMODUS THE CURSE

Commodus wasn't wicked, as such, insisted Dio Cassius, a contemporary commentator, but 'he was a greater curse to the Romans than any pestilence or any crime'. To say that he was eccentric doesn't begin to do justice to his outrageous irrationality. There are good reasons to think that he was, quite literally, insane. And then, combined with the paranoia of so many previous emperors, he had a simple-minded malleability, which made it easy for others to manipulate him to their own malicious ends.

Commodus' reign was accordingly a time of terror, and a time in which political panic and confusion

It went without saying that Commodus expected to be worshipped as a god. He identified especially closely with the deified superhero Hercules.

compromised the effective working of the Empire. Successive conspiracy scares prompted successive purges. In between these, Commodus kept up a fairly constant persecution of the patrician class and the Senate, whose traditional role in government he evidently resented. He himself, with characteristic immodesty, proclaimed his reign a 'golden age'. In reality, wrote the Roman historian Dio Cassius, it was an age of 'rust and iron'.

It went without saying that Commodus expected to be worshipped as a god. He identified especially closely with the deified superhero Hercules. In his

statues – and, of course, there were thousands of them across the Empire – he had himself represented with a giant club, his head draped over with a cloak made of the hide of a lion. This was a reference to the Nemean Lion, ferocious and supposedly indestructible, which Hercules had killed and skinned as the first of his famous tasks. He had always been depicted this way in Roman paintings and sculptures, and so this was how Commodus insisted on being shown. And not just in artistic representations – this was the way the Emperor appeared himself in public.

Just who was he, this strangest, most demented of emperors? One thing he doesn't appear to have been was, in the modern cliché, 'his father's son'. This is the more surprising given that he was actually the first natural son to have inherited the imperial throne since Titus, a century before. Marcus Aurelius was generally agreed to have been pretty much the perfect emperor; Commodus was just about his opposite.

Not surprisingly, his philosopher father had been at pains to ensure that Commodus had all the benefits of an education in academic subjects and in the arts. Commodus was more interested in looking masculine and tough. He was a fanatical follower, and a lavish provider, of gladiatorial shows and liked to associate with gladiators and train with them himself.

SAOTERUS AND THE SENATORS

Unfortunately, Marcus Aurelius doesn't seem to have given his son much sense of duty or responsibility, or any real aptitude for hard work. Commodus was conspicuously idle, quite clearly bored to vexation by the business of government and only too ready to leave it to other people. Chief among his official advisers was Tigidius Perennis, who had been Prefect of the Praetorian Guard under Marcus Aurelius and continued in that position under his son. But Commodus also liked to be able to call on a close companion and adviser for day-to-day decisions. He became reliant on a select few.

Saoterus was the first of these. A Greek freedman, he was the palace chamberlain, but he had made himself indispensable to Commodus, so much so that

Commodus didn't just admire Hercules, he identified with him so closely that he seems sincerely to have believed that he was him. He appeared in the hero's guise in public, carrying a club, and wearing a lion's hide, like that of the Nemean lion killed by Hercules.

THE GLADIATOR

Commodus' macho fantasies extended far beyond his identification with Hercules. He was obsessed with gladiatorial contests, and was desperate to be involved in them himself. Just to be around these professional warriors thrilled him. He gathered them around him and delighted in training with them and hearing their stories. Exhilarated to be in their company, he was a 'man among men'.

As for the gladiatorial show itself, Commodus seems to have been seriously addicted to the adrenalin rush. He spent far more than the Empire could afford on spectacles of this kind. On several occasions, he became so carried away as a spectator that he vaulted the barrier and leapt into the arena so as to join in the action for himself. Of course, no gladiator would dare inflict a significant injury on the Emperor, so the risk to Commodus was actually minimal. They would just go through the motions, allowing themselves to be overcome after the slightest show of a struggle. He didn't mind, though, because he was able to boast that he had outfought some of the Empire's toughest, most skilled gladiators. In return for their cooperation, he would always show mercy to his opponents in their 'defeat', at least in the public arena. Those he fought at home were not so lucky.

Commodus loved to take on wild beasts as well as human gladiators. But dumb creatures didn't understand that he was the Emperor and that they were supposed to let him win, so these contests had to be conducted rather differently. A special platform was constructed running all the way around the arena, with a strengthened balustrade. Commodus could stand here and strike down with a sword at the beasts below, shoot them with arrows or hurl javelins. He could thus claim 'victories' over a wide range of beasts, from lions to rhinos.

Commodus' arrow stops a leopard which has escaped its cage in the arena, one of hundreds of unfortunate animals slaughtered by the Emperor over the years. The whole Empire was hostage to Commodus' enthusiasms, of which his gladiatorial obsession was by no means the most damaging.

Pensilis è cauea Tigris rai
Erumpit vinclis, hominiꝗ occ
4.

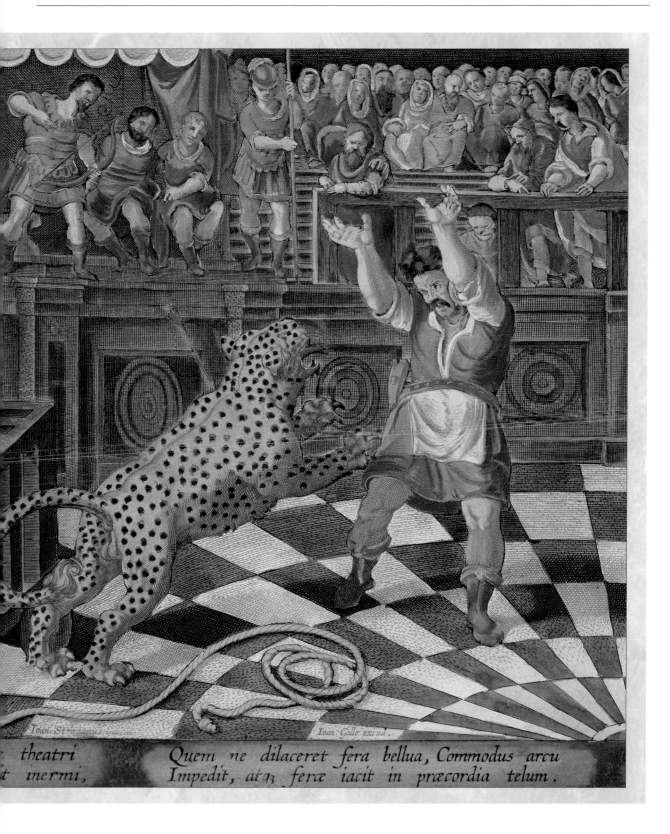

theatri

t inermi,

Quem ne dilaceret fera bellua, Commodus arcu
Impedit, at͑q; feræ iacit in præcordia telum.

An Elaean coin commemorates Commodus: the Emperor is shown riding in triumphant procession, in the manner of a victorious general. In truth he was never much of a soldier: though he served beside his father, he had few achievements in the field of war.

Saoterus was up there alongside his master in his chariot when Commodus made his triumphant entrance into Rome as Emperor in 180 C.E. Thereafter, he remained prominent in the government of the Empire. This outraged the senatorial class, which was systematically sidelined by Commodus. Rome's leading citizens were especially incensed that Saoterus was so obviously not just an adviser but also a lover. Commodus would canoodle with him in public places, which just deepened their disgust, and underlined their impotence.

General patrician discontent became concentrated in Commodus' sisters. They felt the same outrage as the rest of their class, but felt it that much more intimately. They were older than Commodus and resented their little brother's elevation. The most formidable, and the most ferociously bitter, was Lucilla. In 182 C.E., she became the focus of a plot against the Emperor involving Marcus Ummidius Quadratus and Appius Claudius Quintianus, both of whom were her cousins and her lovers.

Bruttia Crispina married Commodus in 178 C.E.: he was a lucky man, it was generally agreed. But not by Commodus himself. Beautiful as she was, her open contempt for him damned her in his eyes. He had her put to death in 182 C.E. on treason charges.

A BUNGLED PLOT

Not for the first or last time in conspiratorial history, a strong woman was let down by inadequate male assistance. Quintianus messed up the assassination completely, and not just by drawing his dagger too soon as he dashed up to Commodus to deliver his death blow. As he strode forward, too focused on his target to realize that the Emperor's bodyguards were closing on him, he yelled out, 'This is the message I bring you from the Senate.' So, not only was he caught before he could strike the Emperor, but also he had revealed the existence of a wider conspiracy, even before he had been tortured. He was executed, of course. Quadratus was also put to death. Lucilla, her daughter, and a sister of Quadratus who had also been involved were sent off to exile on the island of Capri.

So, too, was the Emperor's wife, Bruttia Crispina, even though there was really no evidence to suggest that she had been a part of the conspiracy. But why not? Commodus had never liked her. She was famous for her

> Quintianus messed up the assassination completely, and not just by drawing his dagger too soon as he dashed up to Commodus to deliver his deathblow.

beauty, and her family connections had made her a good match when he wed her in 178 C.E., but her disdain for her husband had always been apparent. Commodus' mercy towards these female conspirators seems to have been solely for public show. A few months later he had all four of them quietly put to death.

One unexpected victim of this plot was Saoterus, whose envious rivals saw their chance to remove him from the scene. Another freedman, Cleander, who had risen high in the imperial administration, got sympathetic members of the Praetorian Guard to

arrest the Emperor's pet, on the grounds that he had been involved with the conspiracy. It was nonsense, of course. The chamberlain had the Emperor exactly where he wanted him. How could he conceivably have benefited by having him replaced? But Saoterus was never to have the chance to state that case. Cleander had him summarily put to death.

PERENNIS PROFITS

Commodus was said to have been more furious at this than he had been at the conspiracy itself, but Cleander knew exactly how to handle his imperial master. He soothed away his anger and managed to persuade him that it had all been an innocent misunderstanding. Appointed to Saoterus' position as chamberlain, he began to worm his way into the Emperor's affections himself.

Perennis was the man of the moment, though. He secured his position as Commodus' key adviser by pretending to have discovered a new conspiracy. This one, he claimed, was led by Tarrutenius Paternus, the man who just happened to be Perennis' rival for leadership at the head of the Praetorian Guard. He had also, in fact, been an important player in Lucilla's

A CHARMED LIFE

One woman got clean away with her role in the conspiracy against Commodus. This was Marcia, mistress of Senator Ummidius Quadratus. She had been a prime mover in the plot, but she was so successful in acting the innocent that, far from being executed, she was made the Emperor's mistress. She continued to hold on to Commodus' affections with her winning ways, and after Crispina's exile and death she was practically his wife.

It was Marcia who softened the Emperor's irrational rage against the Christians. She seems to have been a follower of the new faith herself. She persuaded Commodus to call back from exile hundreds of Christian believers who had been sent to slave in the mines of Sardinia, thus saving them from what amounted to a death sentence.

Commodus' statue was to be seen everywhere, his imperial cult energetically promoted. The reality was that, increasingly, he was leaving the responsibilities of ruling to favoured officials and devoting his life to the pursuit of pleasure and to his games of gladiatorial prowess.

conspiracy, but had escaped undetected, so it could be argued that a sort of rough justice was being done. But Perennis' real motivation was, of course, the destruction of a competitor: Paternus and several of his friends were now put to death.

A LIFE OF EASE

Commodus was relieved to hear that this 'conspiracy' had been nipped in the bud, and he was further reassured by Perennis' insistence that he now relax. The conduct of the Empire was safe in his hands, the Prefect promised. Commodus had no need to bother himself with the ins and outs of government. Why not devote his time entirely to pleasure?

Commodus needed no second invitation. He had the Empire combed for its most beautiful girls and women and they were brought to his palace to form a harem 300 strong. A similar number of youths was collected to act as servitors and attendants – and, of course, the Emperor's lovers as required. He held vast banquets at which every kind of debauchery was committed. He bathed with all his companions, male

> Commodus had the Empire combed for its most beautiful girls and women, and they were brought to his palace to form a harem 300 strong.

and female. He liked to watch as his various women and others were violated by youths. Lucilla was dead by now, of course, but Commodus' other sisters were made his concubines. He even bestowed the name of his own mother on one of his mistresses.

And then there were his sporting interests. Commodus spent more and more of his time in the country, at his estate near Lanuvium, to the southwest of Rome. There he could ride and drive his chariots and spar with gladiators to his heart's content, going

A BIT OF A WIT

Commodus never really grew up, and his hostility towards the Senate, Rome's official government, was often brutal. But it sometimes took on an air of boyish mischief, such as the time when the Emperor got the senators to vote him funds for an official visit to North Africa so he could blow the whole lot on banquets and on sports.

But his wit could have a cruel streak. Once, it's reported, tickled by the sight of a few odd hairs sprouting from a bald man's head, he said that they looked like worms wriggling up out of the bare ground. He went as far as having a starling brought and placed on the man's bare head. The bird was taken in by the illusion, and pecked away at the unfortunate victim's crown until it was raw and turning septic.

Although a noted glutton himself, Commodus took childish pleasure in poking fun at fat people. One man was so fat that the Emperor insisted his stomach be split open to see what happened. What did happen, of course, was that all his guts spilled forth and he died a slow and agonizing death.

Commodus was intrigued by the cult of Bellona, the goddess from Asia Minor whose worship was introduced to Rome during his reign. Its adherents slashed at their arms with blades at the climax of their religious frenzy. The Emperor considered it amusing to prevent this by cutting off their arms.

Commodus also thought it was witty to make fun of the physically handicapped. He would give lame men a head start and then 'hunt' them, taking shots at them with bow and arrows. Sometimes he had them handicapped. On occasion, he would have a victim's foot cut off or eye gouged, then delight in calling them names like 'one-foot' or 'one-eye'. He pushed his Praetorian Prefect and his retinue, fully dressed, into a bath.

The young Commodus (left) was celebrated for his looks, but this seems only to have heightened his general tendency towards narcissism. His sadism singled out the adherents of the Asian goddess Bellona (right), whose cult was just catching on in Rome during Commodus' reign.

He did not see the funny side where slights to himself were concerned. He had quite a temper, too, when things didn't go exactly as he wanted. When he was only 12, he flew into a rage when his bath wasn't quite hot enough. He demanded that the slave who had prepared it be thrown into the furnace, but was fooled when a sheepskin was put in instead. The stench of burning flesh convinced him that his order had been carried out, and the condemned man lived to draw a bath another day.

Cõment les germaniés et les gaulliés se departiret de lepereur comodus et de seu empire ~
Capptrle .j.

Puis die que au comme chement de ceste presente oeuure nous

anons determine apaele des nobles princes qui en harmau ont eult leur prince prinapalment et ens es tamps de lenpereur comodus toutte franche tant superiore comme Ju

As imagined by a medieval monk, the Emperor tells his senators – seen here in fifteenth-century churchmen's garb – about the revolt by Germans and Gauls against his latest tax demands. Even by imperial Roman standards, Commodus was extravagant: his profligacy put a strain on the Empire as a whole.

into the nearby town to see shows and sporting events from time to time.

And so he whiled away his days and nights in an endless round of idleness and dissipation, while Perennis made himself the real master of the Empire. The Prefect wielded his power ruthlessly, having his opponents tortured and put to death, and confiscating their estates. Like Domitian, Perennis concocted what amounted to fictional conspiracies, just so that he could have the alleged participants executed and help himself to their possessions. He amassed enormous wealth at the expense both of private citizens and the state. Commodus would not hear a word against his Prefect. He was just delighted to have someone else attending to his duties. Anyone who did brief against Perennis would almost certainly soon be dead.

But the Prefect was mistaken in assuming that his position was unassailable. He went too far when he started grooming his own son for the imperial succession. And he made it all too obvious, upsetting not just the Senate but also many in the army, when he started passing off other generals' victories as his son's. Cleander, who, although biding his time, had certainly not surrendered his own ambitions, saw this as his moment to make a move.

CLEANDER CLEANS UP

In 184 C.E., the chamberlain gave a group of officers access to the Emperor to voice their complaints. They had been serving in Britain, and felt bitterly aggrieved. As far as they were concerned, the credit they were due for the services they had done the Empire had effectively been stolen from them by Perennis and his son. Commodus may not have been too bothered about who had earned what tribute in faraway Britain, but he saw very clearly the agenda the Prefect was pursuing right there in Rome. He promptly gave the order for Perennis to be put to death.

That left Cleander sitting pretty as the Emperor's sole confidant and chief of staff. He took personal charge of the administration of the state. His lust for power put Perennis' in the shade as he set about seizing all the Empire's offices. Anyone who tried to obstruct him, he destroyed. But it was his rapacity for wealth that took the breath away. Everything was for sale: senatorial status; provincial governorships; military commissions; tax inspectorates. You name it: in Cleander's Empire it had its price. You could overturn a court conviction by paying the imperial chamberlain the required bribe. All the officials had paid for their positions anyway.

And his influence was only growing. As Cleander's corruption began to compromise the functioning of the Empire's institutions, the year 187 C.E. saw widespread discontent. In the army, especially, there was anger, with legionaries deserting in large numbers, especially in Germany and Gaul. One officer, Maternus, a leader of the mutineers, made his way to Rome to assassinate the Emperor. He was caught and

> You name it: in Cleander's Empire it had its price. You could overturn a court conviction by paying the imperial chamberlain the required bribe.

executed, though. Rather than blaming Cleander for causing all this trouble, Commodus was full of gratitude to the man he felt had saved his life.

A few months later, there was another plot. This time, one of the Emperor's brothers-in-law, Antistius Burrius, and his friend Arrius Antoninus, conspired to kill not just Commodus, but Cleander as well. Pertinax, another of the Emperor's high officials, a man with high ambitions of his own, discovered the would-be assassins.

CORRUPT PRACTICES

For the moment, though, Cleander went from strength to strength. In 188 C.E. he had Perennis' successor as Prefect executed on trumped-up treason charges and took personal control of the Praetorian Guard. In 190 C.E., no fewer than 25 new consuls were nominated. There had never been anywhere near so many before. Cleander pocketed an enormous payment for every last one of these appointments,

although he reserved the right to have the new official put to death if he ended up crossing him in any way. As ever, Commodus was happy to know that somebody else had taken charge, but Cleander was also careful to cut Commodus in on the proceeds of his corruption.

A SPECTACULAR DOWNFALL

In the end, Cleander, too, was brought down, by a dangerous combination of natural disaster, popular anger and patrician guile. When, in 190 C.E., a crop failure suddenly reduced the supply of food, grain commissioner Papirius Dionysius saw his chance to undermine the Emperor's right-hand man. The shortages were causing real suffering in Rome. Far from doing his best to find alternative sources elsewhere in the Empire, Dionysius shut off the flow of food completely. Cleander had caused the famine by his systematic looting of the Empire, the commissioner hinted. He knew he could rely on the mob to do the rest.

> Commodus ordered that Cleander be executed there and then. Seizing upon his body, the crowd carried it away with them. Someone cut off the head and it was placed upon a pole and paraded triumphantly through the streets.

The people seethed for days and weeks, but popular anger finally boiled over one afternoon in June, when huge crowds had come together in the Circus Maximus. A horse race was actually in progress when a tall young woman, gaunt and grim in her expression, strode into the stadium leading a large group of children. They wailed with hunger and yelled out complaints against Cleander. No one knew who the woman was. Many concluded afterwards that she had been a divinity of

This tablet, recording a ruling on a dispute over city boundaries for tax-gathering, dates from 177 C.E., a time when Commodus was co-reigning with his father, and was therefore actually attending to such workaday responsibilities. Put solely in charge, Commodus allowed his Empire to descend into a mire of corruption.

some sort. Undeniably, her impact on the afternoon's events was remarkable. The crowd at large, who went off to find the Emperor, took up the children's protests.

Cleander responded by sending the Praetorian Guard against the mob. At this point, though, Pertinax decided to show his true self. He had been Cleander's rescuer a few years before, of course. Now, though, he felt ready to rise higher. He dispatched a troop of soldiers to face down the guardsmen Cleander had called out. All of a sudden, the Emperor's preferred man was on his own. Apart, that is, from the angry multitude doggedly pursuing him, which finally caught up with him at the house where he had sought sanctuary with the Emperor. Commodus was dumbfounded, and shaken to see the determined mood of the populace. He simply sat there, paralyzed with terror. Fearing for his life, and urged on by Marcia, his mistress, he decided to give the people what they wanted. He ordered that Cleander be executed there and then. Seizing upon his body, the crowd carried it away with them. Someone cut off the head and it was placed upon a pole and paraded triumphantly through the streets. The people then turned on those officials they saw as having helped Cleander in his robbery of Rome. Several were dragged roughly from their homes and lynched.

A POLICY OF PANIC

At a loss without his chamberlain, Commodus now took charge himself for a brief but chaotic few weeks in which supposed plotters were executed willy-nilly. Papirius Dionysius didn't get to enjoy his satisfaction at bringing down Cleander for too long. His role was identified and he was put to death. So too was Julianus, the new Prefect of the Praetorian Guard, just a few days after he had been appointed. Commodus' aunt Annia Fundania Faustina was accused of conspiracy and killed, as was Mamertinus, his brother-in-law.

Soon, though, order was restored. Quietly, in the background, Marcia was taking hold of the situation. The Emperor's mistress complemented him perfectly. Where he was idle, cowardly and ineffective, she was a woman of enormous courage and competence. She was helped by the fact that Commodus' new chamberlain, Eclectus, wasn't primarily driven by a desire to further his own interests. At last, there was a team at the top that Commodus could rely on. Trust the Emperor to go and blow it for himself.

The sense of at last being in control of his Empire seems to have gone straight to Commodus' head. His grasp on reality, always shaky, was weakening fast. What had once seemed little foibles became fixed delusions. He was starting to accept his own propaganda as true. He literally believed he was Hercules, honestly believed that he was a god. He absolutely believed that he had taken on 12,000 gladiators and won. He had a plaque inscribed to that effect and publicly displayed beneath his statue. He saw no reason why Nero should have his colossal statue outside the Colosseum (moved there from the *Domus Aurea* some years before). So he had the head lopped off and replaced with his own, with a Herculean lion-pelt cloak, of course, and a club was added to the sculpture too.

ABSURD EXTRAVAGANCE

Commodus was capricious, suddenly calling for this or that official to be taken off and executed. He became absurdly extravagant in his whims. One afternoon, at a moment's notice, he decided that 30 races would be run at the Circus Maximus in just two hours. Rome was grinding to a halt. What with all the Emperor's games and gladiatorial shows, no one in the city was really getting any work done. No matter. Commodus in his bounty was handing out sums of money to the populace on impulse. And to encourage the people to share his view that his reign had inaugurated a 'golden age', he ordered a general lowering of prices.

The movie *Gladiator* (2000) was loosely based on the life of Commodus, with Joaquin Phoenix playing the Emperor's part. Here he questions his sister, Lucilla (Connie Nielsen), whose loyalty he has started to suspect. Not without reason: she is scheming to bring about his downfall.

There was little love lost between Lucilla (right) and her brother Commodus. She would have resented his authority, even if he hadn't used it to make her marry against her will. In the end, she conspired to have him killed – only to be executed for her pains.

All this generosity meant that he had to find other ways of raising revenue. This too he tended to do on impulse. He abruptly announced that the entire senatorial class – every man, woman and child – would have to give him two gold pieces each as a birthday present. Similar arrangements were introduced across the Empire. More sinister, like Domitian, he dreamt up imaginary conspiracies so that he could have the alleged participants put to death and could then confiscate their property for his use.

BEYOND ALL REASON

Towards the end of 191 C.E., Rome was hit by another great fire, which left much of the urban interior a smoking ruin. Commodus was unperturbed. It seems to have been at this point that he had his great idea of establishing a new city, a new civilization in his own name. So it was that, in 192 C.E., came *Dies Commodianus* ('Commodian Day'), when he refounded Rome as a new colony and ordered that all of its people should bear his name.

Those around the Emperor were getting really worried now, because they no longer felt sure they could manage his moods and manias. Where was all this madness going to end? Marcia was horrified when, on the evening of 31 December 192 C.E., her husband told her his plans for bringing in the New Year. It was customary for the Roman Emperor to show himself in public outside his palace in his imperial toga, trimmed with purple. But Commodus was going to break with tradition, he said. Beside himself with boyish excitement, he confided that he was going to make his appearance with his friends the gladiators, marching forth from their barracks geared up for the arena. What more stirring sight could there possibly be?

Commodus was deeply upset and angry when, rather than crying out with glee at this proposal, his mistress burst into tears. Flinging herself down on her knees before him, she begged him not to disgrace the Empire with such a stunt. The Emperor, peeved, went off to complain to his most trusted advisers, Eclectus, his chamberlain, and Aemilius Laetus, the new Prefect of the Praetorian Guard. To his fury, they agreed with

Marcia and begged him not to carry out his plan. He stormed off in a rage, vowing to have his own back on them for this betrayal. Commodus was in deadly earnest. He added all three names to the list he had already drawn up for another group of senators to be executed the next morning.

While the Emperor was in his bath, his young pageboy-lover wandered in and chanced to pick up the wax tablet the list was inscribed upon. It was bound in brass and wood, so an attractive object in itself, and the boy wandered off with it as a plaything. Marcia met him and, worried that he might accidentally erase whatever was on his master's tablet, took it from him. There she saw her name atop the list of those to die.

A DESPERATE REMEDY

Stunned, shaken and finally enraged, she swore that she would see if a drunken sot like Commodus could get the better of a sober woman like herself. She called Eclectus and Laetus and told them of her discovery, and they all agreed that the Emperor had to die. As

'Hail Caesar! We who are about to die salute you!' This scene was acted out at the start of every gladiatorial show. Although first and foremost a bloody entertainment, such contests were also a ritual reminder of the Emperor's life-and-death authority over his subjects.

Marcia, like any other loving mistress, was accustomed to bringing Commodus a drink of wine in his bath, it was the easiest thing in the world to administer the poison there and then.

Commodus felt fuddled, but at first assumed it was the effect of his hot bath and the warm wine. Peacefully, he began to fall asleep. Only afterwards did he go into convulsions and start vomiting. At this point, the conspirators flew into a panic, fearing that he might rid his stomach of the poison. They stood irresolute, wondering what to do. Narcissus then came into the room. He was a professional wrestler and Commodus' fitness coach. They promised him rich rewards if he would dispatch his master physically. The deal was done. Narcissus bent over and finished off the Emperor by strangulation. This 'curse' upon the Romans had at last been lifted.

CHEATED OF REVENGE

There was rejoicing in the Senate when the news of the Emperor's death was announced. It was said to have been the result of an apoplexy. There were calls for Commodus' body to be dragged through the streets and tossed into the Tiber. There were then howls of outrage when it transpired that Pertinax had cheated them of their triumph by having the late Emperor secretly buried in the night. Some demanded that he be dug up so that his corpse could be given the ignominious treatment it deserved. In the end, though, calmer counsel prevailed, and Commodus' body was left to decay in peace.

The Senate still had the satisfaction of declaring that the *Colonia Lucia Annia Commodiana* was once more to be known as Rome. It also pronounced a *damnatio memoriae* ('damnation of the memory') upon the dead Emperor. Every trace of this monster would be erased, every picture and statue of him destroyed, so that it would be as though his reign had never happened. But that was easier said than done. So many statues and inscriptions had Commodus commissioned across the Empire, and so many scars had he left upon so many hearts and minds.

The curse is lifted. Commodus meets his fate at the hands of his fitness coach Narcissus. The intention was actually to poison him, but his murderers, led by Marcia, his mistress, worried when he started vomiting that he would empty his stomach and compromise their plan.

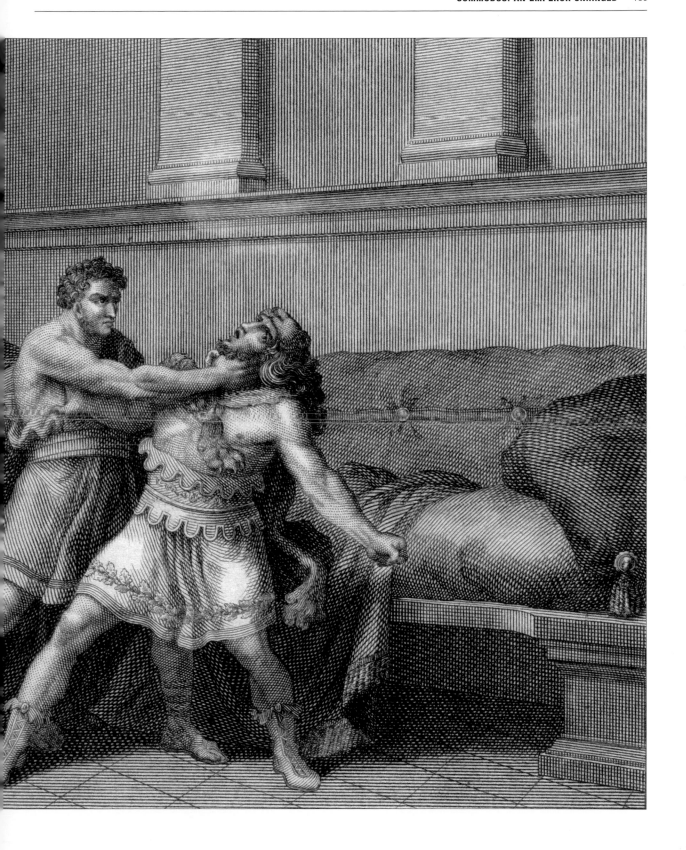

193: ROME'S YEAR OF SHAME

After Commodus came chaos: the imperial throne was up for grabs, its occupants hostages to their so-called protectors in the Praetorian Guard. In the end, Septimius Severus took charge: a tough soldier and a man of action, he seized power for himself and restored order to the Empire.

◆

Now what to do? The decision to assassinate Commodus had been taken instantaneously. The 'conspiracy' had taken shape in a matter of minutes. Once Marcia had chanced upon the death list, she and her fellow advisers had been left with no alternative. It had been either the Emperor or them. There had certainly been no long-term strategy, no plan for what was to happen after Commodus' death, and no candidate had been chosen for the succession. The obvious man was Pertinax. He was regarded as

Despite the dignified air of his official portrait-bust, Commodus had been an apology for an emperor: having practically bankrupted the Empire during his reign, he left it divided and in disorder. It took years for Septimius Severus to reintroduce some sort of discipline.

being a 'safe pair of hands', even though he had shown his skills as a political tactician.

RELUCTANTLY ACCLAIMED

On 1 January 193 C.E., Pertinax was taken to the headquarters of the Praetorian Guard outside the city. There he addressed the troops, calling on them as Romans to rally round and support the Empire in its time of crisis. At this point, the idea was that they would enthusiastically hail him as their Emperor. In the event, though, that isn't quite what happened. That Pertinax had proven his competence and courage was neither here nor there. The Guard didn't like the sound of his plans to restore rational government to Rome.

Commodus may have been a monster and a madman, he may have practically bankrupted the

BOGEYMAN BEYOND THE GRAVE

If Pertinax found it hard to get the Praetorian Guard to acknowledge him, he had still more trouble asserting his authority across the Empire. When the messengers bearing the news of his accession arrived in the various provincial capitals and made their announcements, many of them were arrested and imprisoned on the spot.

It wasn't that the governors didn't welcome the news. What a relief it would be to have a half-rational emperor! It was just that, after so many years with a madman on the throne, they didn't dare believe their luck. It would have been all too typical of Commodus to stage his own death deliberately, to test the loyalty of his provincial administrators. If they allowed themselves to be tempted into acclaiming this supposed successor, wouldn't Commodus come out of his hiding place and spring his trap?

Their fear of offending the new Emperor was as nothing to the abject terror they felt for the old one. It was several days before they could be persuaded that Commodus was really dead.

Empire, but his spendthrift generosity had won him real popularity with the people. A fair bit of that largesse had come the way of the Praetorian Guard, and they had no desire to see an end to this open-handedness. Pertinax, however, was a serious statesman talking earnestly about the need to address the abuses of the previous reign, for radical reforms to the economy and for belt-tightening. It wasn't what the guardsmen wanted to hear.

Pertinax was no fool. He saw the ranks of stony faces looking back at him and knew he was going to have to try a change of tack. He offered them all a sizeable *donativum* or 'gift', a whopping bribe by any other name. That was much more like it. A ragged cheer went up, and Pertinax got the all-important endorsement he had sought. His acclaim had still been half-hearted, though. The Guard distrusted his economizing instincts. They weren't sure about him, so he was going to be an Emperor on probation.

HAPPY ENDINGS?

Now that Commodus was gone, Marcia married Eclectus, her fellow slave. Some said that they had been lovers for some time. They had certainly been through a great deal of trauma together at the heart of the imperial household. Now they looked forward to settling down to a happy married life. It was not to be. Pertinax decided that their decision showed great presumption on their part as slaves and promptly had them taken out and executed. It could well be, of course, that he didn't want two such formidable operators alive and potentially interfering as he sought to establish his authority as Emperor.

It was already clear that this was going to be something of a struggle. Pertinax might be in power, but he was no nearer his own happy ending. His position was very difficult all round. The people hadn't

> If they allowed themselves to be tempted into acclaiming this supposed successor, wouldn't Commodus come out of his hiding place and spring his trap?

wanted him, partly because they didn't know him and partly because what little they did know was that he planned to cut back on the 'bread and circuses' they loved. Their hostility left him dependent on the backing of the Praetorian Guard, which was growing less enthusiastic by the week.

He was finding it hard to get together the money he had been forced to promise the Praetorian Guard. He sold the contents of Commodus' palace to raise funds.

Clever, capable and ready to be ruthless when the occasion demanded it, Pertinax might have made a successful ruler in another age. But so badly had Commodus' reign corrupted Rome that the Emperor's task was impossible: he was seen simply as a source of bribes for his Praetorian Guard.

IMP · CAES · DIVI ·
M ANTONINI PII GERMANICI
SARMATICI FILIVS · DIVI ·
COMMODI FRATER ·
DIVI ANTONINI PII NEPOS DIVI HADRIAN ·
PRONEPOS DIVI TRAIANI PARTHICI ·
ABNEPOS DIVI NERVAE ADNEPOS ·
L · SEPTIMIVSSEVERVS
PIVSPERTINAX AVG ·
ARABICVS ADIABENICVS P · MAX ·
TR · POT · IIII IMP · VIII · COS II P · P ·
COLVMNAM VII TEMPESTATE
CONFRACTAM · RESTITVIT ·

An inscription celebrates the life of Septimius Severus, Rome's Emperor from 1 June, 193 c.e. There have been greater rulers, but there is no doubt that the Libyan-born military man had the qualities needed at the time to bring an anarchic Empire back under control.

There were gold-embroidered silken robes, fur-trimmed cloaks and rich clothing of every kind, gemstone-encrusted weaponry, precious drinking cups and sumptuous dining ware, stunning ceramics, beautiful ornaments, breathtaking jewels and beautiful chariots. And not just these inanimate treasures, but also Commodus' human property. This included his male and female concubines, his misshapen cripples, his dwarves and his clowns. They were all slaves, so they, too, could be auctioned off to the highest bidder. Everything had to go. This imperial sale may have represented one of the more ignominious moments in Roman history, but still it wasn't enough to raise the amount of money that was now needed.

HELD TO RANSOM

Even if Pertinax had succeeded in paying the Praetorian Guard the amount he'd promised them, it seems unlikely that this would have kept them quiet for long. The truth was that Commodus had used them to mount a sustained assault on the patrician class, and they had grown accustomed to having a great deal of power and plunder. The new Emperor's instincts were obviously to run a peaceful Empire on sound economic principles, founded in enlightened social policies and sensible reforms. It just wasn't going to be a natural environment for what had become little more than an army of freebooting thugs.

And besides, for all his good intentions, Pertinax had crossed an important boundary when he had offered the Praetorian Guard their *donativum*. Emperors up to now had stabbed and poisoned their way to power, but no one had actually bought the throne. If Pertinax had done that this time, why wouldn't another candidate do it next time? A deeply unfortunate precedent had been set.

PRAETORIAN POWER

Early in March, Pertinax made a visit to Ostia to review the arrangements for grain shipments to the capital. He was very much the conscientious, 'hands-on' ruler. While his back was turned, however, a group of rival senators and military officers attempted a coup under the leadership of the consul Quintus Sosius Falco. The Praetorian Guard did what it had been paid for. The plot was discovered and the conspirators executed, but the weakness of Pertinax's position was underlined.

> Commodus's property to be sold off included his male and female concubines, his misshapen cripples, his dwarves and his clowns. They were all slaves, so they too could be auctioned off to the highest bidder.

Later that same month, just 87 days into Pertinax's reign, the Praetorian Guard abandoned all pretence of loyalty. The guardsmen marched on Rome in a body, and launched a full-scale assault on the imperial palace. Sent out to negotiate, Laetus lost his nerve and threw in his lot with the attackers. Pertinax's advisers urged him to flee and save his life. But the Emperor was naïve enough to trust in his powers of persuasion. He would reason with the Guard and explain why he was governing the way he was. the plan was noble, and it nearly worked. The assembled soldiers were impressed by Pertinax's courage and his conviction. Business was business, though, and they cut him down and killed him.

AN EMPIRE FOR SALE

Having taken possession of the palace, the Praetorian Guard now, quite openly and quite literally, let it be known that the office of Emperor was for sale. Whichever man was to offer them the highest sum of money for the position would have the Guard's full backing as possessor of the throne. If Pertinax's sale of the palace furnishings had seemed unworthy of the dignity of the Empire, what were the Roman people meant to make of this?

And yet, the squalid auction went ahead. Pertinax's father-in-law, Titus Flavius Sulpicianus, was keen to keep the office in his family. He bid 20,000 sesterces for every soldier. This was a fabulous sum, but it was easily surpassed by Didius Julianus' bid of 25,000. He,

·DID·
IVLIANVS

Left: Little is known of Didius Julianus apart from the ignominious fact that he – quite literally – bought the office of Emperor. Within weeks of his accession he had been overthrown by Septimius Severus: the guards he had paid so much did not lift a finger to save him.

accordingly, won the backing of the Guard. The Senate protested, but they were helpless to resist the bullying of the Praetorian Guard. So it was that, on 28 March 193 C.E., the Emperor Didius Julianus was officially proclaimed. His wife and daughter were both awarded the honorific title of '*Augusta*'.

   We know practically nothing of what sort of Emperor he was, or might have been. His brief reign was completely overshadowed by the controversy over his election. While it would be nice to be able to report that Romans were outraged on principle, that wasn't the whole story, by any means. The populace seems to have

> The people did not accept their new Emperor. They jeered at him contemptuously and pelted him with stones when he showed himself in public.

been shocked by what had happened. They had been impressed, despite themselves, at Pertinax's integrity as Emperor. And even if they hadn't quite come to love him yet, they were still appalled to see him hacked down by his own guard in his own palace. To see his throne then put up for sale was beyond the limit.

A CONFUSING COUP

The people did not accept their new Emperor. They jeered at him contemptuously and pelted him with stones when he showed himself in public. He quickly learned to stay safely in his palace. That being the

Right: Another claimant to the imperial throne, Clodius Albinus was Governor of Britain when he heard of Didius Julianus' elevation. He made an alliance with Septimius Severus against Pescennius Niger, the commander of the eastern armies – but both men were looking to outmanoeuvre one another.

THE VIRGIN SOLDIERS

For someone who had bought the imperial throne, Didius Julianus was strikingly starry-eyed and idealistic. He was a true romantic where Rome and its traditions were concerned. As Septimius Severus advanced on the city with his army, and the Senate looked to him for leadership, he proposed that the Vestal Virgins be sent out in procession to meet the invasion force.

Wearing white gowns, they would hold out fillets or headbands before them, the conventional posture of those pleading for mercy since the days of the Trojan War. They would beseech the oncoming soldiers to respect the inviolability of Rome, their ancient home and the mother of the Empire.

Not surprisingly, this suggestion was greeted with guffaws. What loyalty was Septimius Severus likely to feel towards a Rome being ruled by Julianus? And why should his soldiers (many of them barbarians) feel any reverence to such values? But Plautius Quintilius, consul and priest, was downright contemptuous when he declared that no man had the right to possess what he was not prepared to defend by force of arms.

case, he was fairly soon forgotten. When all was said and done, the people were used to doing as their masters told them, so after a few days' restlessness their rage subsided.

If anarchy continued across the Empire, that was because, as in 69 C.E., the 'Year of the Four Emperors', important power groups felt they were missing out. Military commanders were incensed at seeing the political initiative being taken by a group they didn't even look upon as proper soldiers. The Praetorian Guard was just a jumped-up personal protection unit. Why should they have all the power, and all the spoils?

Three generals independently rose up with their troops against the new regime. Clodius Albinus was the Governor of Britain. Far to the east in Syria, not

> The last thing the Praetorian Guard saw themselves as was a serious fighting unit. Still less did they feel a sense of patriotic loyalty to Rome.

just his own troops but also those in Egypt and Asia Minor had proclaimed Pescennius Niger Emperor. Again, as in 69 C.E., distinctive regional power blocs were emerging, a recipe for disunity and continuing

The vestal virgins were the priestesses of the temple of Vesta, goddess of the hearth and home, and thus the living embodiment of the eternal spirit of Roman femininity. No true Roman would dream of insulting them – increasingly, however, the Roman legions were no longer made up of Romans.

chaos. Septimius Severus had been born in Africa, in what is now Tunisia, and, like Lusius Quietus, he was the son of a Berber chief. He had enlisted in the Roman army, though, and risen spectacularly through the ranks to his current post as commander in Pannonia (roughly, modern Hungary).

SEVERUS PROCLAIMED EMPEROR

No sooner had his legions heard the news of Didius Julianus' enthronement than they proclaimed their own commander Emperor of Rome. He headed westwards towards Italy and Rome. There, Julianus was trying to mobilize the Praetorian Guard to defend the capital, but they were most reluctant to take their stations. For years now they had seen their primary function as pushing the patrician class around on behalf of the Emperor, and latterly they had taken upon themselves the right to bully the Emperor himself. Steeped in cynicism as they were, though, the last thing the Praetorian Guard saw themselves as was a serious fighting unit. Still less did they feel a sense of patriotic loyalty to Rome.

So it was that, on 1 June 193 C.E., Septimius Severus was able to march into Rome with his army without meeting significant resistance. The Senate

acknowledged him as Emperor. The helpless Julianus was arrested and beheaded. He had been on the throne for just over two months. The new Emperor showed the Praetorian Guard who was boss by abolishing it altogether, and executing those who were thought to have led the conspiracy against Pertinax. Septimius Severus created his own elite guard, drawn from his loyal legions, to replace it.

CIVIL STRIFE

The fighting was by no means over. Septimius Severus might have been recognized in Rome, but as far as the east was concerned Pescennius Niger was Emperor. Clodius Albinus, meanwhile, controlled a vast segment of western Europe, including not just Britain, but also all of Iberia. Septimius Severus, who even awarded him the imperial title of Caesar, acknowledged his authority in those territories. It was understood that, although the African might be Emperor for now and for as long as he lived, Clodius Albinus would have the claim to his succession. The two agreed an alliance as Septimius turned his attentions to the east, marching his army out to engage the eastern 'Emperor' and his legions.

They met at Cyzicus, northwest Turkey. Niger's army, now outnumbered, was forced to retreat. Much the same happened a few weeks later at Nicaea (Iznik), a little further east. In 194 C.E., however, Septimius Severus followed through, dealing his rival a crushing defeat at the Battle of Issus. Niger fled to the east, hoping to find sanctuary with Rome's Parthian enemies, but was caught and killed. His severed head was sent back to be exhibited outside the walls of Byzantium. The city had sided with Niger in the recent fighting and still remained defiant. Severus displayed Niger's head as a warning to its occupants of the fate awaiting them.

UNDER SIEGE

Unfazed, they prepared to resist, and Septimius Severus' army settled down for a siege. It was not going to be easy, they knew. Byzantium's situation was superb from the defensive point of view. It was high up on a headland around which fast currents create constant turbulence. Its ports were walled, their entrances controlled by boom-chains which could be raised or lowered to admit shipping, or to keep it out. Long breakwaters extended out into the sea on either side, on which archers could easily be positioned so

that any hostile ships approaching would have to run the gauntlet. The city's fortifications – massive walls, with high, protruding towers – were said to be the most formidable in the ancient world. Archers standing on these could cover the walls and ramparts at will, showering arrows down upon attackers.

GUERILLA TACTICS

At intervals along the walls, moreover, were engines of every kind, including catapults and ballistae (giant crossbows). Defenders could lob huge boulders or wooden beams at their attackers or send heavy bolts hurtling toward them, and often these would be tipped with blazing fire. Ships incautious enough to approach the walls were liable to find themselves hooked like fishes because hooks were abruptly lowered by pulley systems so that vessels could be yanked out of the

---

In 194 C.E., Septimius Severus dealt his rival Pescennius Niger a crushing defeat at the Battle of Issus. Niger fled to the east, hoping to find sanctuary with Rome's Parthian enemies, but was caught and killed.

---

water. The Byzantines' own naval strength was considerable. They possessed 500 galleys with hardened bows for ramming the enemy. Many of them had rudders both fore and aft to maximize movement at close quarters.

The Byzantines used guerrilla tactics too, sending divers down under cover of darkness. They would drive bolts into the sides of Roman ships and attach long cables. Then, cutting the anchor chains, they would signal to their comrades on the walls. Again, like anglers, they would 'reel in' their catches. In short, between the strength of all its various ways of

Pescennius Niger enjoyed widespread support among the legions on the eastern frontiers, who named him as Emperor in 193 C.E. Ultimately, however, he was out-generalled by Septimius Severus, who defeated him at the Battle of Issus in 194 C.E. then caught and killed him.

defending itself and the determination of its garrison, Byzantium was well nigh impregnable.

But its people had to eat. That, Septimius Severus realized, was the point of vulnerability. He set to work sealing off the city from the outside world. Starving it into submission was harder than he had expected, though. It didn't help that opportunistic blockade runners would slip through with fresh provisions for the besieged. They knew that those inside the city would pay top rate for food. If the Romans caught them and challenged them on this, they would claim to

The head of Septimius Severus, captured in cold marble. There was a certain coldness about the living man. Having coolly got the better of him in a game of divide-and-rule, he had the head of his rival, Pescennius Niger, paraded on a pole.

have been 'captured' by the Byzantines and forced to give up their cargoes against their will.

Eventually, though, the blockade began to bite, and hunger to gnaw at the insides of the defenders. An air of quiet hysteria took hold. They still defended bravely. When the ammunition for their giant catapults ran

GOOD FORTUNE

Rome's first African Emperor had an Aramaean wife. Julia Domna was the daughter of a Syrian priest from Emesa (now the town of Homs). Septimius Severus was Governor in eastern Gaul when he decided that he simply had to marry her, even though he'd not yet met her, and didn't even know her family.

What he *did* know was that everyone was saying that an astrologer had told this girl that one day she was going to be a queen. And that was really all the ambitious Severus needed to know about her.

She was still a teenager, while he was already a widower in his forties, but they seem to have got along together from the start. Ferociously bright and competent, she was also formidably brave and tough, and she went with her husband on many of his campaigns.

Later, when he was in power, the Empress stayed at home and looked after things while her husband went off to fight enemies and put down rebellions. Rome's traditional elite didn't like it much, but of course neither Severus nor Julia were themselves Roman, and they were unconcerned by patrician disapproval.

Septimius Severus and Julia Domna made an odd couple, but a well-matched one. Both were outsiders, of Libyan and Syrian antecedents respectively. The future emperor had married her on a superstitious whim, but they had become inseparable companions, with Julia even accompanying her husband on his campaigns.

out, they hurled stone sculptures and bronze statues and other things instead. They repaired their increasingly tatty ships with timbers torn from houses. They even replaced frayed ropes with new ones braided from their women's hair.

THE BITTER END

They fed themselves, after a fashion, by soaking hides until they were soft enough to chew, and this miserable fare was enough to keep death at bay for many weeks. But resolve was ebbing away. The general populace was in rebellious mood, yet, even now, they did not think of surrendering. Instead, a large number launched a mass breakout. One night, when a vicious storm whipped up the waters of the Bosporus and they knew the Romans would never dream of putting to sea to stop them, they set out across the straits in their small boats. Many were lost, of course. Those who survived were in a near-demented state. They attacked the first villages they came upon, plundering for food.

For those left behind in the city, the future looked grim indeed. They now faced certain starvation. Some bought themselves some extra days and weeks by resorting to cannibalism. Others attempted a second mass escape by boat. Again, stormy conditions appeared to work for them, but their vessels were crammed full with refugees, so they lay low in the water, and many were immediately swamped as soon as they reached open waters. They were certainly too sluggish to escape the pursuing Romans, who this time had been ready and resolute. They sailed among the Byzantine craft, ramming them and spilling their human cargoes into the waves, or snaring them with grappling hooks and dragging them under. Looking down from the battlements above at what seemed a sea of bodies and broken boats, the Byzantines finally despaired of outlasting the siege and offered their surrender.

WINNER TAKES ALL

With the threat from Pescennius Niger removed, Septimius Severus no longer had any need for his alliance with Clodius Albinus. Immediately after the Battle of Issus, he had named his own son, Caracalla, as his successor. He was surely not surprised when, far to the west, Albinus' legions reacted by proclaiming their general Emperor and started getting ready to

move on Rome. Septimius Severus marched his men northwards to intercept Albinus's men.

They met near Lugdunum, now Lyon, in central France, on 19 February 197 C.E. Severus had been occupied for much of the intervening period dealing with the Byzantines' obstinate resistance. And besides, it had taken months for the two contenders for the Empire to organize, equip and provision the enormous armies with which they hoped to secure the throne. Fittingly, with such a prize at stake, it was one of the greatest battles of ancient times.

> They fed themselves, after a fashion, by soaking hides until they were soft enough to chew, and this miserable fare was enough to keep death at bay for many weeks.

As many as 150,000 men are believed to have taken part. The two forces were roughly evenly matched, both in numbers and determination. The advantage seesawed back and forth as they slugged it out over two whole days. Casualties were very heavy on both sides. In the end, though, Severus' cavalry was able to give him the edge, sweeping down into Albinus' exhausted infantry. Their resistance was finally broken, and Albinus fled.

HEADS ON POLES

His cause clearly lost, the would-be emperor threw himself upon his sword so as not to suffer the humiliation of being captured. Cheated of this triumph, Severus ordered that the body be beheaded and then stretched out upon the ground. Before his watching army, he then rode his horse furiously back and forth over his vanquished rival. He had Albinus' head, along with those of his family, sent to Rome to be displayed on poles as a warning to others.

Septimius Severus rides back and forth over the dying body of Clodius Albinus to underscore his emphatic triumph at Lugdunum in 197 C.E.. He went on to have Albinus' family killed and their heads displayed on poles. The message was clear: this soldier-emperor would brook no rival.

CARACALLA AND GETA :
THE FEUDING EMPERORS

**No brotherly love was lost between Caracalla and Geta, Septimius Severus'
sons: they squabbled and bickered incessantly from boyhood up. Their
enmity might easily have pulled the Empire apart completely, but before
that could happen Caracalla had his younger brother murdered.**

◆

Septimius Severus had won himself an Empire in upheaval. Everywhere he looked, there was restlessness and disorder. Since Commodus' death at the end of 192 C.E., Rome had been distracted by its own internal conflicts. Local administrations had been losing their grip without really noticing. What were tribesmen to do in Spain or Britain while their Governor mobilized his legions for his leadership bid? Wait quietly until normal colonial service was resumed? What of a Middle Eastern client king? Was he simply to carry on collecting Rome's taxes and administering its

Septimius Severus' strong hand brought an anarchic empire back under control, but it failed him when it came to his own sons. It was an error to name Caracalla as his successor at so early a date, guaranteeing years of rancour from the younger Geta.

laws as though nothing was happening? And what of Rome's external enemies? Should they hold off their attacks until Rome was ready?

The answer, of course, was that none of these people did anything of the kind. Emboldened by a general sense that Roman rule was significantly weakening, they took whatever advantage they could. The Empire was too strong, well ordered and tightly regimented to fall to pieces just like that. But even so, when Septimius Severus completed his victory over Clodius Albinus in 197 C.E. and became undisputed Emperor, he found himself facing a wide range of challenges.

AN ABSENTEE EMPEROR

That suited him, in fact. He had always been a soldier first and last. He liked being Emperor, but he was never happier than when he was in the field, which was just as well. He was to spend the greater part of his reign conducting a series of 'fire-fighting' operations. In some ways, it suited the Empire too. Given some of the shenanigans of the past few years, it was good to feel that the army was being kept constructively occupied by a military strongman, the sort of tough-talking, tough-acting Emperor who really could command the troops' respect.

But it did leave the Roman capital without its Emperor for long periods of time. This was no problem, as far as Severus was concerned, because he had full confidence in his wife's capacity to take charge. And he was right. Julia Domna was probably the most gifted and conscientious administrator the Empire had ever had. She also did a great deal to enhance the prestige of Rome. An important patron of the arts, she invited writers, artists and philosophers to the imperial court. The leading thinkers of the day genuinely respected her opinions. She possessed one of her generation's most distinguished minds.

> The Empress was a political operator of the utmost skill. She was instinctively adept at playing her opponents off against one another, and nimbly evaded the traps they tried to set.

If her higher intellectual skills were impressive, so was her low cunning. The Empress was a political operator of the utmost skill. She was instinctively adept at playing her opponents off against one another, and nimbly evaded the traps they tried to set. There was always someone trying to catch her out, to get her to say something unguarded or overstep some mark, but Julia never gave anyone that satisfaction.

She also had the support of Gaius Fulvius Plautianus, Severus' cousin, lifelong friend and right-hand man. Although of Roman descent himself, Plautianus had been born in the Emperor's African hometown of Leptis Magna. They had got to know each other in boyhood and stayed close. In 197 C.E., Septimius Severus appointed Plautianus Prefect of the Praetorian Guard. Between them, Julia and

Plautianus were capable of coping with just about any eventuality. The Emperor knew he was leaving his capital in safe hands.

UNSTABLE SONS

Rome got by just fine without Septimius Severus, but unfortunately, the same could not be said of his two sons. Lucius Bassanius, the elder, had been born in 186 C.E., so he had been just seven when his father first seized power in Rome. Publius Septimius Geta was three years his junior, but the two brothers argued from an early age. How much this went beyond the usual sibling rivalry isn't clear. However, things took a dramatic turn for the worse once Septimius Severus became Emperor.

Suddenly, the stakes were raised. Lucius was named as his father's successor, and was renamed Marcus Aurelius Antoninus. The former Emperor had helped Septimius Severus' career along, and it was he who had made him a senator in 172 C.E. But Lucius' re-branding was clearly designed to suggest a familial connection that didn't actually exist. If the implications of the new name were bogus, there was no doubting what they meant for Geta. His brother was going to rule the world, so what was he going to do?

What had been a difficult, conflict-ridden relationship from the start now became seriously toxic. Geta regarded 'Antoninus' with the deepest loathing. 'Antoninus' fully reciprocated those feelings, and then some. As he grew older, 'Antoninus' was to be renamed once again, when he was universally known as 'Caracalla', from the kind of hooded Gallic cloak he liked to wear. But it didn't seem to matter what he was called. Geta hated him by whatever name, while he in turn couldn't hide his contempt for his younger brother. It was all their mother could do, in between her million-and-one administrative duties, to prevent her sons murdering each other.

PLAUTIANUS IN POWER

Wrapped up as she was in the unending task of trying to mediate between the boys, Julia seems to have eased

An obliging sculptor portrays the young Lucius Bassanus, or Caracalla, as the infant Hercules, strangling snakes: as far as he was concerned, the most menacing serpent was his own brother. The destructive struggle between them poisoned not just their own relations but the political life of the Empire as a whole.

He looks imperious enough in his official portrait bust, but Geta had not apparently been born to rule. That fact, and the arbitrary destiny which had reserved the Empire for his elder brother, drove Geta all but insane with envy and frustration.

off in her administrative duties to some extent. From 197 C.E. onwards, Severus' friend Gaius Fulvius Plautianus took on more and more of the responsibility for running the state. Inevitably, the Praetorian Prefect was also amassing power and, increasingly, wealth. This was fair enough. The Emperor rewarded him by making him consul, and he even had his image represented on Roman coins.

But Julia was growing alarmed. Although some were comparing Plautianus to the earlier Sejanus, he seemed if anything more ambitious than Tiberius'

treacherous lieutenant. The Prefect had more statues in the city and around the Empire than most emperors had done, and they were bigger than any emperor's as well. He was conducting himself like a ruler, and a ruthless one at that, having those who opposed him assassinated or executed at will. He was living as luxuriously as any eastern potentate in history. It wasn't difficult, when the provinces paid their tribute directly to him. He was ransacking the Empire, and robbing the Emperor, just as surely as Cleander had done in Commodus' reign. But Septimius Severus wouldn't hear a word said against his friend.

> Gaius Fulvius Plautianus was conducting himself like a ruler, and a ruthless one at that, having those who opposed him assassinated or executed at will.

Aware of Julia's reservations about his rise, Plautianus did his best to bring her into disrepute. He had her servants and friends arrested and tortured in hopes of exacting some damaging testimony against her. But the Empress' friends were loyal, as was her loving husband, who dismissed the idea that his wife might pose him any threat. Yet his affection for his old friend didn't weaken.

A MATRIMONIAL MISMATCH
The two men cemented their relationship through a marriage alliance, arranging that Severus' elder son Caracalla should take Plautianus' daughter Fulvia Plautilla as his wife. The bride brought with her a dowry that would have satisfied 50 queens. The wedding was spectacular, arranged as it was to coincide with the festivities for Severus' tenth anniversary as

Her husband's helpmeet, Julia Domna tried her hardest to be there for her sons as well, but their hatred was just too violent and all-consuming. Julia's political instincts were sure, her cunning and courage legendary, but the task of reconciling her two sons was to prove quite beyond her.

PRESERVING PLAUTILLA'S REPUTATION

Plautianus wasn't just power-crazed. He was becoming crazed in a more general sense. Nothing illustrates that better than his raising of his young daughter. Publia Fulvia Plautilla, to give her full name, had been born in 188 or 189 C.E., so she was in her early teens by the time her father's power was coming to its zenith.

Plautianus wanted his beloved daughter to have every advantage of education and social polish, so he surrounded her with teachers and attendants of the highest class. She was given tuition, not just in writing and philosophy, but also in music and the arts. Plautianus made sure she had the best-qualified men to instruct her in all these things.

But the Prefect was also obsessed with the idea that her chastity had to be protected, and he didn't trust his fellow men an inch. So he had them all castrated, not just the slaves but also the high-born teachers and companions, and not just the young boys, but also the bearded men. In all, it's said, he had a hundred grown men gelded, all of patrician birth, and all for the sake of his daughter's virginity.

Plautilla, Plautianus' beloved daughter, was marked out for marriage to Caracalla from an early age, although the match was to prove a disaster for all concerned. Caracalla, coerced into marrying her, never tried to hide his hatred: he ultimately had her executed with her family for treason.

Emperor and for all his recent victories. Severus was just back from the Middle East, where, after prevailing over the Parthians, he had put down a number of insurrections in Mesopotamia and Palestine.

Plautianus paid for the main entertainment in the Colosseum, in the course of which 60 savage wild boars fought one another to death. But the climactic moment came when a large wooden structure in the shape of a ship was drawn in on rollers. Suddenly the sides fell away and 400 wild animals rushed out. There were lions, leopards, panthers, wild ass, bison and ostrich running madly around the arena. Squads of gladiators danced and dodged among this milling mob of terrified beasts, attacking and killing them to the delight of a cheering crowd.

The bride and groom do not appear to have had any fun at all. This wasn't so much an arranged marriage as an enforced one. Caracalla had begged his father not to make him marry Plautilla, but Severus had remained unmoved. What Pautilla's feelings for her husband were we do not know, but they can hardly have been all that warm, given how utterly and how openly he despised her. Plautilla was only about 15 when she was wed, which wasn't at all unusual for a Roman girl. It was stranger, though, that Caracalla was only a couple of years older. So disgusted was he with his match that he would barely acknowledge Plautilla as his wife. This was to be a marriage made in hell.

PLAUTIANUS AND THE PLOTS

Plautianus had been pleased at the idea of having his daughter married to Severus' son. It would secure his position at the very top of the imperial establishment, he believed. His connection with Caracalla would ensure that he remained a power at the Emperor's court not just through Septimius Severus' reign, but also through his son's. But that had been before he realized quite how unwilling a bridegroom the young man was going to be, and how intensely he would hate his wife and father-in-law thereafter.

Far from coming round, Plautianus now realized, Caracalla nursed a deep and implacable loathing that showed absolutely no signs of weakening over time. As for keeping his Prefecture in Caracalla's reign, Plautianus could forget that. Would he even survive once Severus' protective presence had been removed? That was the question he found himself pondering now. If he was in any doubt about the answer, it was

removed when Caracalla started issuing a stream of death threats against him. Ultimately, it was in a spirit of defending himself that the Prefect set in motion a plot to overthrow Septimius Severus, kill his family and seize the throne of the Roman Empire for himself.

He was only playing into the hands of Julia and Caracalla, both of whom had now got wind of what he was planning and had been organizing a conspiracy of their own. They warned Septimius Severus, and Plautianus found himself summoned to a meeting with the imperial family at the palace. There he was challenged on his treachery because extensive details of what he had been doing had been discovered.

Not without some sadness, Severus had him put to

> So disgusted was Caracalla with his match that he would barely acknowledge Plautilla as his wife. This was to be a marriage made in hell.

death. A *damnatio memoriae* was pronounced and all his statues and inscriptions were destroyed. He was being erased from the record of Roman history. His property was confiscated and his family banished to Sicily. Since that included his detested wife Plautilla, Caracalla was well pleased with his work. (Seven years later, when he was Emperor himself, he would have his executioners finish the job. Plautilla, her brother and his daughter were all strangled.) Plautianus was replaced as Praetorian Prefect by Aemilius Papinianus, a relation of the Empress from Syria, but a famous authority on Roman law.

SAME OLD SAME OLD

Plautianus had ended up dominating the first decade of Septimius Severus' reign. Now the imperial family was once more firmly at the heart of the Empire. That wasn't altogether a good thing. Thrown back on their own devices, they encountered all the same old problems, and the same old tensions and resentments were surfacing. Without his wife and father-in-law to enrage him, Caracalla remembered how much he hated Geta, who had spat blood at seeing his brother freed from the hell of his married life. Julia resumed her struggle to stop them fighting.

Suddenly footloose and fancy-free, Caracalla threw himself into a life of debauchery. Geta had to compete in this, as in all else. As though vying with one another to see which could behave the more outrageously, they violated women, sexually assaulted boys, embezzled money and spent it without restraint. Like Commodus, they took to hanging out with gladiators and charioteers. Once they competed in a chariot race, and Caracalla was thrown out and broke his leg. In keeping such rough company, they seemed to be rebelling against their parents and turning their backs on official life. They did involve themselves in Roman politics, but only as a means of pursuing their feud. Invariably, they lined up with opposing factions.

Julia snatched Geta in her arms and tried to protect him. Horrified, she felt the lifeblood bubbling out of her beloved son as he was hacked to death in her embrace.

SHOW OF UNITY

The more the brothers squabbled, the harder their parents worked to keep up the show of unity. They felt it was crucial that the imperial family was seen to be as one. So when, in 208 C.E., Septimius Severus had to travel to Britain to put down unrest among the natives, his wife and sons all went with him. Papinianus went along, too, in hopes that he might help to keep the peace. But the arguing continued without pause, and eventually their stay in Britain ended badly after the Emperor caught a severe fever.

Before he died in Eburacum (York), on 4 February 211 C.E., Severus begged Papinianus to be a guardian to his sons. The Prefect and Julia Domna both promised to do all they could to try to heal the rift between Caracalla and Geta. It was their father's wish that they should rule together, but their reign was a disaster from the start. Neither could contain his contempt for his co-ruler. Caracalla, who had expected to be his father's sole successor, was furious to find himself double-crossed, as he saw it. And Geta felt no

His father's anointed successor, Caracalla was not perhaps the perfect choice as Emperor: his instability went well beyond his lifelong feud with his younger brother. His marriage, too, became a draining, destructive hatred. Caracalla's hostility towards his wife was second only to his loathing for his brother, Geta.

gratitude for an Empire he was going to have to share with his hated brother.

IN HIS MOTHER'S ARMS

Back in Rome, the tension between the two became unbearable. Sacrifices were offered to Concord, the goddess of harmony and agreement, as well as to the other gods and goddesses, asking for divine intervention to bring the brothers to make peace. But all to no avail. It was an open secret that Caracalla was plotting his brother's death. Geta made his own plans, motivated both by his hatred for his brother and his desire to kill Caracalla before he himself was killed. Caracalla had intended to make his move during the noise and confusion of Saturnalia, the festival of Saturn and the Roman equivalent of the modern Carnival. But this became such common knowledge that he was forced to abandon the plan – so heavily guarded was Geta now, no assailant could get close.

Then an even more devious stratagem came into Caracalla's mind. On 26 December 211 C.E., he sought a meeting with his mother Julia. Telling her in tones of heartfelt sadness how much he regretted his foolish feud with his younger brother, he begged her to attempt her conciliator's role once more. With tears in her eyes, she agreed, and sent a message to her younger son to come, without his attendants, for a private meeting in her chamber.

But Caracalla had paid some soldiers who were waiting outside her apartment. As soon as they heard that Geta had arrived they came rushing in. Terrified, the young man rushed to his mother and cried out to her to save him. She snatched him in her arms and tried to protect him. Horrified, she felt the lifeblood bubbling out of her beloved son as he was hacked to death in her embrace.

A LIKELY STORY

There was almost an established procedure by now for what an imperial murderer had to do. Caracalla went straight to the barracks of the Praetorian Guard. He explained to the troops that he had been forced to act

AN UNCERTAIN ASSASSIN

Caracalla's heart seems to have been almost consumed by his rage against his younger brother, but he still managed to save some hatred for his father. It suddenly surfaced one day when, at a crucial moment of Severus' Scottish campaign, a group went to negotiate the surrender of a Pictish tribe. As the massed ranks of the Roman legions stood waiting, the party rode out before them. At its head was Septimius Severus himself. Caracalla kept him company, beside and just a little way behind him. The Emperor's bodyguard was trailing some paces back.

It must have been this fact that caused the idea to occur Caracalla that this was to be his moment of destiny. Abruptly reaching for his sword, he drew it and raised it high above his head ready to ram it into the body of his father. From behind came a bodyguard's startled shout, and at that point Caracalla became conscious that what he was doing could be seen by many hundreds of Romans, not to mention several perplexed-looking Picts.

Caracalla sheathed his sword, and, as though absolutely nothing had happened, Septimius Severus rode on, and the ceremony of surrender went ahead. Only when they were back at the camp that night did the Emperor call Caracalla in to see him along with Papianus. He took his sword and handed it to the young man.

He was old now, the Emperor said, and could easily be killed by a determined attacker. If Caracalla didn't dare to do the deed itself, why not ask Papinianus to do it for him? He was young and strong enough to do what was required. And, as a loyal servant of the imperial household, he would not dream of disobeying an express order. Why not give that order now, if that was what Caracalla wanted? Caracalla had an assassin's hatred, but not an assassin's courage. In silence, he dropped his gaze and shook his head.

The aged Emperor Septimius Severus rebukes his son Caracalla for seeking to assassinate him: murderous hatred was the norm in this most dysfunctional of families.

Although his father's heir-apparent, marked out for unlimited power and unimaginable wealth, it seemed Caracalla could never find contentment. His running battles with just about everyone – his brother, his wife, his father and even his mother – suggest someone at odds with his own self.

because Geta had been plotting his assassination. No one believed a word of it. That was clear.

There was anger. In fact, several of the guardsmen insisted that this time they had sworn to defend two Emperors, not one. Geta deserved their loyalty as much as Caracalla did, and they should avenge his death, however illustrious his assassin. It was touch and go for a time, but then Caracalla remembered the procedure. He promised the Praetorian guard a massive *donativum*, or financial 'gift'.

> It wasn't as easy to defend a brother's murder as it was to carry it out. It was a brave reply, but not a tactful one. It cost Papinianus his life. He was to be just one of many.

A BROTHER'S RAMBLINGS

The Senate wasn't going to be so easily squared. They listened with undisguised disbelief to Caracalla's ramblings about his younger brother's treachery. He was going to have to do better. To that end, Caracalla went to Papinianus and asked him to give a speech explaining why he had been forced to act as he had. The distinguished lawyer refused. He might be famed for his oratory, but he wasn't up to a challenge like this. It wasn't as easy to defend a brother's murder as it was to carry it out. It was a brave reply, but not a tactful one. It cost Papinianus his life. Again, Caracalla claimed his victim had been conspiring to kill him.

A REIGN OF TERROR

Papinianus was to be just one of many. In the end, the Senate supported Caracalla because they simply didn't dare do anything else. The Emperor was unbalanced and utterly unrestrained in his rage. In his zeal to wipe out Geta's faction and all those connected to it –

The rivalry between Caracalla and Geta ran so deep that it was perhaps inevitable it should have a tragic end – and so it did, with the younger brother's brutal murder in 211 c.e. This painting by Sir Lawrence Alma-Tadema depicts the brothers at the Coliseum, eyeing each other suspiciously.

Caracalla was crazy, but an Emperor's insanity had the force of law: he raped a Vestal Virgin, then charged her with impurity. That meant burial alive, sealed up inside an underground chamber to starve, so that her blood would not be on the city's hands.

however tenuously – he had no fewer than 20,000 people killed. In the face of such a spree, it didn't make sense to resist. Caracalla was too frightening, and also too unpredictable.

He had many of Rome's leading citizens murdered, not because they were scheming against him, but simply because he envied the admiration in which they were held. He played games, building men up by appointing them to the highest positions in the state before knocking them down, killing them and their families and confiscating their estates. He was torn. He wanted achievers around him, but always ended up envying them what they'd done. Invariably, he would end up killing them. That went for a succession of friends and confidants as well. He became dependent on their advice and support, then found himself resenting that dependence.

HERO WORSHIP

Alexander the Great, the greatest military leader of ancient times – perhaps of any time – fascinated Caracalla. This is not of course surprising in itself. Alexander's father, Philip II of Macedon, had been a formidable military ruler, like Septimius Severus. No one had dreamt that his son could come close to matching his achievements. In the end, though, Alexander had far surpassed them. It was easy to see why his example might have been a comforting one for Caracalla to keep in mind.

He collected memorabilia, including weapons, drinking cups and other items said to have once belonged to the great man. He had busts and statues of Alexander everywhere. He read everything he could find on the subject. He had some elephants fitted for war because the conqueror had used these in his Indian invasion. He even maintained what he called his 'Alexander's Phalanx'. Its 16,000 Macedonian troops were kitted out in exactly the same fashion as Alexander's

infantry and carried the same *sarissa* pikes that they used. Some 5m (16ft) long, these were topped with a wickedly curving blade. Caracalla's Macedonians were fully drilled in its use and so were able to go into action in exactly the manner of Alexander's army, half a millennia before.

Perhaps the oddest aspect of Caracalla's 'Alexander-mania', however, was the irrational hatred of Aristotle that went with it. The famous philosopher had been Alexander's tutor as an adolescent, and there was an extremely improbable story that he had been involved in some way in his master's death. Caracalla declared war on Aristotelian philosophers, breaking up their academies and burning books.

In the third century B.C.E., Alexander the Great had conquered most of the known world. Caracalla's admiration of the Macedonian was carried to excessive – and eventually to downright murderous – extremes.

Having bought the support of the army with big wage increases across the board, he found himself faced with the problem of how to pay them. In desperation, he debased the currency by reducing its silver content by one-quarter, so he could mint more coins to meet commitments. It was the height of economic folly. The only way he could see of backing up his debased currency with greater wealth was to expropriate the property of the patricians. Like Domitian, then, Caracalla embarked on a sustained persecution of the Empire's leading citizens, trumping up charges of treason and embezzlement against them.

He oppressed and assaulted as he pleased. Having raped one Vestal Virgin, he then had her buried alive as a punishment for her 'impurity'. Three other young women died with her, even though he knew them to be

The Egyptian port of Alexandria was one of the great cities of the Roman world – here we see what remains of its splendid theatre. But its citizens were unfortunate enough to fall foul of Caracalla: many thousands ended up paying with their lives.

The Baths of Caracalla were one of the architectural glories of ancient Rome, although what happened inside was somewhat shabbier, moralists suggested. Bathhouses had always been places where prostitutes picked up their clients. With its mixed bathing, this one was little better than a brothel, it was claimed.

innocent. He insisted, however, that they had committed acts of lewdness.

THE RAPE OF ALEXANDRIA

Caracalla couldn't take a joke. Despite his admiration for Alexander the Great, he was to order a horrific massacre in the metropolis his hero had founded at the mouth of the Nile, all because of a satire he found to have been circulating in the city mocking his claims that he killed his brother to defend himself. Although enraged, he managed to contain his fury. Instead, calmly and cold-bloodedly, he sent Alexandria's leading citizens a message expressing his warmest regard and announcing his intention of making an official visit.

When his ship docked in the Egyptian port and the city fathers appeared to welcome the visitors, he

invited them to share a banquet. Caracalla did them proud, entertaining them in the most lavish imaginable manner, with endless amounts of the finest food and wine. Finally, he served up a surprise dessert. At a discreet signal, his armed men streamed in and put the Alexandrian worthies to the sword.

SITTING DUCKS

That was just the start. While the banquet had been going on, Caracalla had been landing a whole army, and this force was now commanded to go into the city and place it under curfew. All its citizens were to be confined to their homes. Far from being safe there, they were sitting ducks ready to be slaughtered as Caracalla's soldiers worked systematically through the city from house to house. More than 20,000 of Alexandria's leading citizens were massacred, their property plundered, their bleeding bodies flung

---

Like so many others in Roman history, Macrinus faced a straight choice: kill or be killed. There was only ever one choice he was going to make.

---

together into common graves. Foreigners were expelled and the city turned into an armed camp, with walls built to prevent people passing from one sector to another.

Caracalla didn't just kill the people. He also trampled all over their traditions. He was brazen enough to dedicate his deeds to Serapis, the deity who had traditionally protected Alexandria. A Greek version of Osiris, the ancient Egyptian god of life and death, Serapis had his high temple in the city. There it was that Caracalla took up residence while his troops were carrying out their atrocities. He even offered up the weapon with which he'd had his brother killed as a sacrifice at Serapis' altar.

THE BATHS OF CARACALLA

The most striking achievement of Caracalla's reign was his construction of the baths that bear his name. In fact, to talk of the 'Baths' of Caracalla doesn't do justice to the ambitious scale of this gigantic complex or the number of different facilities it offered.

It was by any standards an impressive building. Inside, its magnificence took the breath away. Well over 1500 people could be in the various baths at any one time. There were hot pools and cold plunges, as well as warm *tepidaria* for idling in. Serious swimmers could thrash up and down the *natatio*, the swimming pool. But there was a lot more to the baths than bathing. Such as the two large *palaestra* or gyms, for example, the outside running tracks, the indoor shopping mall or the large library (with books in both Latin and Greek). All in all, the complex offered everything needed to uphold the Roman ideal of *mens sana in corpore sano* ('a healthy mind in a healthy body'). Just how healthy it was from a moral point of view, some commentators of the period ventured to doubt. The Baths became a notorious pick-up place for prostitutes.

PROPHET OF DOOM

Caracalla's moods were so unpredictable, his deeds so erratic, that it's a wonder he managed to reign as Emperor at all. That he did so was thanks largely to his Prefect of the Praetorian Guard. Marcus Opellius Macrinus had first come to prominence in the service of Septimius Severus, but was Caracalla's second in command. His rise was remarkable not only because he was a Berber, but also because his family had belonged to the 'equestrian' class. The *equites*, or 'horsemen', were so called because they had traditionally provided the Roman army with its cavalry. Socially speaking, they were a cut above the lower class from which the foot soldiers were drawn. There was still a significant gulf, though, between the equestrians and the upper-class patricians, so Macrinus had obviously done very well.

So well that, inevitably, his rise attracted a great deal of gossip. What really worried Macrinus, though, was something that sounded as if it should have been good news. It was reported that a soothsayer had prophesied that Macrinus would rise even further, and that one day he would actually be Emperor. Far from being pleased at this prediction, Macrinus flew into a panic. He knew predictions such as this would be his death sentence, once they reached Caracalla's ears, because Caracalla wasn't going to sit back meekly and allow himself to be overthrown. He would have Macrinus murdered without delay.

Caracalla came to a cruel end at the hands of his own bodyguard, cut down by a roadside, far from Rome (above). If Macrinus (right) did not actually order Caracalla's assassination, he was its obvious beneficiary, but he was to have little joy in his succession.

Already, the Emperor had started reorganizing his staff, moving key officials from positions under Macrinus and replacing them with new ones. Was this simply interference on Caracalla's part, or a stage in a deliberate plan to undermine him and perhaps to bring about his death? Like so many others in Roman history, Macrinus faced a straight choice: kill or be killed. There was only ever one choice he was going to make.

LAST STOP

Caracalla was campaigning on the Empire's eastern frontier when 217 C.E. began, fighting yet another war against the Parthians. Macrinus was there as well, with the troops of the Praetorian Guard, because it was their job to protect the Emperor wherever he was.

One afternoon in early April, a small party went with Caracalla to worship at a temple to Luna, the Roman

ON THE GAME

Rome is famous for its legions, but it had an army of prostitutes as well, from high-class courtesans (*delicatae*) to common *noctiluae,* or 'night walkers'. Whole professions doubled as prostitutes, including mime actresses (*mimae*) and cymbal players (*cymbalistriae*), as well as bakers' girls (*aelicariae*) and barmaids (*copae*). There was even a category of whore who hung around in cemeteries and graveyards, and the *bustuaria* would also hire out her services bumping up the number of mourners at a funeral if required.

There was no law against prostitution in ancient Rome because the founding fathers, in their patrician haughtiness, had decided that there didn't need to be. Their reasoning was circular. Selling your body was such an indignity that being a prostitute was a punishment in itself. Aristocratic wives who were unfaithful were publicly disgraced because their crimes were seen to have brought disrepute on their families. Ordinary streetwalkers had no status, so were beneath the notice of the authorities and could accordingly be safely left alone.

The Romans had a rich and varied brothel culture, with a variety of categories ranging from the big *lupanares* to the tiny *turturillae* ('dovecotes') or *tuguria* ('cottages'). Some of the largest brothels seem to have been regimented almost along industrial lines, with dozens of women in rows of little cubicles or stalls. (This seems to have been the kind of place in which, according to the gossip, Claudius' wife Messalina had gone to work.) There were also *casuaria* (roadhouses) along all the main highways and *tabernae* (inns or taverns) in the cities. Some were extremely discreet. Others, such as the celebrated *pergulae*, had outside balconies on which women posed and beckoned to passers-by.

For the prostitute, working in one of these places had its obvious attractions because it offered a degree of protection and support. Roman society fully accepted the paying patron's right to beat up (even to kill) a prostitute whose services he wasn't satisfied with, so women were always facing a degree of risk. But many women either couldn't get into such

A madam and her customer do the deal, as depicted in a tombstone from the 3rd century C.E. A veritable industry in ancient Rome, prostitution had a semi-respectable status: a sex-entrepreneur would have seen no reason to be ashamed of her success.

establishments or chose not to. They didn't like the degree of supervision it involved, or they resented having to hand over a cut of anything they earned.

The result was that many prostitutes plied their trade independently. Many met their clients in quiet side streets and dark alleys. For greater shelter and seclusion, though, there were always the arcades around Rome's great amphitheatres or the halls and passageways of the city's public baths. There had been public baths almost as long as there had been Romans, but in Republican times separate facilities had existed for the different sexes. The mixed-bathing policy prevailing at the newer complexes such as the Baths of Caracalla was effectively a green light to prostitution.

moon goddess. The shrine was special because it stood near the spot where the Battle of Carrhae had been fought in 53 B.C.E. Julius Caesar's friend and fellow Triumvirate member Crassus had suffered a major

---

> As Caracalla struggled to get back up on to his horse, one of his bodyguards came up, apparently to help him. Instead, he slid his sword into his guts.

---

defeat at the hands of the Parthians, but it was always important to pay tribute to the Roman dead.

That evening, as they rode back towards their camp, Caracalla needed to answer the call of nature.

The party drew to a halt, and he dismounted and urinated by the roadside. As he struggled to get back up onto his horse, one of his bodyguards came up, apparently to help him. Instead, he slid his sword into his guts. That, at least, was the version given by Macrinus when he and his men arrived back at the camp with the bodies of the Emperor and his alleged assassin. In his fury, the Prefect said, he had attacked and killed Caracalla's murderer. That, of course, meant that the soldier's story could not be heard. Whether he had really killed the Emperor we will never know. But one thing is quite certain. Macrinus was the main beneficiary of Caracalla's murder.

The Baths of Caracalla reduced to a romantic ruin – a fitting monument to this thwarted emperor. Caracalla's reign had been compromised from the first by his all-consuming hatreds; by the uncontrollable resentments that crowded out his capacity for rational decision-making.

ELAGABALUS: A TEENAGE REPROBATE

The competition is fierce, but the conclusion is inescapable: no emperor was more spectacularly unfit for imperial office than Elagabalus. So wrapped up was he in his tormented sexual obsessions, his mad lust for luxury, that he barely gave his official responsibilities a thought.

✦

Macrinus proclaimed himself Emperor. He hadn't set out to seize power to start with, but one thing had led to another and here he was. Once he was on the throne, though, he very quickly got used to it. He gave his son Diadumenianus the title 'Caesar' and named him as his successor. The Senate was happy enough to have Macrinus because, despite his humble background, he had always shown due respect for Rome's traditional elite.

As for the ordinary people, they didn't know what to think. It has to be remembered that this drama was

Now an ageing matriarch, Julia Domna remained a force in Rome, struggling hard to keep the Severan Dynasty together. With her help, the family was restored to power, but in the person of Elagabalus – a young man beyond all reason and all control.

acting itself out hundreds of miles away in the east, where the war against the Parthians was continuing. It all seemed unreal to begin with, but then, as the months went by, they became increasingly resentful that they'd still seen neither hide nor hair of their new Emperor. The court had relocated to Antioch, the main focal point in the province of Syria and for the moment a sort of acting capital for the Empire.

THE JULIAS GET ORGANIZED

All the usual politicking and intriguing had been transplanted here. At the hub of the action was Julia Domna. She'd been a major influence on two successive emperors, and although both of these were now dead, along with her younger son, she wasn't in a hurry to give up her hold on power. And this was despite the fact that she was slowly and agonizingly being wasted by a serious illness (now believed to have been breast cancer). As determined as ever, and backed up by her younger sister, Julia Maesa, she did all she could to make life difficult for Macrinus. He finally ended up ordering that both women be banished from Antioch.

HUNGER STRIKE

Julia Domna refused to go. Sick as she was, she did not feel capable of making a move, nor did she see any reason in her present state to fear death. Instead, she stayed in her apartments and steadfastly refused to take any food. Within a few weeks, she had starved herself to death. Julia Maesa went back to the sisters' birthplace, Emesa, to lick her wounds.

> It was obvious that the officials Macrinus had placed in charge were unable to cope, and the buck stopped with the Emperor himself.

At another time, this would have seemed a serious hardship. In normal circumstances, Syria was a long way from the core of things. Right now, though, with persistent trouble on the frontier, the energies of the Empire were all being directed eastwards. Far from feeling exiled, removed to the political margins, Julia Maesa drew strength from being on her home ground.

She could also rely on the staunch support of her daughters, two more Julias, Julia Soaemias and Julia Mamaea. They were both strong, ambitious women, like their mother and their aunt, and they shared the same powerful sense of destiny. If they were down, for now, they certainly weren't out. In Emesa, far from retiring, they spent their time plotting to recover their family's lost power. Julia's eunuch adviser, Gannys, who became tutor to Julia Soaemias' son, Varius Avitus Bassianus, gave the women additional advice.

REVERSALS EAST AND WEST

She can only have been encouraged by the news that was coming in from both east and west. The war against the Parthians was going badly. Later that same

Macrinus was barely in power long enough to make it onto the Empire's currency, it might be thought. But here he is, on a coin issued in Ephesos. He was a skilled politician, but no match for the Julias, who quickly contrived his downfall and his death.

summer, Macrinus' army suffered a heavy and humiliating defeat, and he was forced to make a huge payment to the Parthian king to get him to withdraw. This wasn't the Roman way of doing things, as the army was all too well aware. There was growing discontent with Macrinus' rule.

In Rome, meanwhile, anger over the Emperor's absence only grew when a terrible thunderstorm struck the capital. While lightning set several of the taller tenements ablaze, torrential rains filled the sewers and drains to overflowing and the city was hit by a double whammy of fire and flood. It was obvious that the officials Macrinus had placed in charge were unable to cope, and the buck stopped with the Emperor himself.

Julia Soaemias has the dubious distinction of having been mother to the future Emperor Elagabalus – her family fostered the rumour that he had been born of an affair with Caracalla. They renamed the boy 'Marcus Aurelius Antoninus' to reinforce the idea that this was a natural succession.

Elagabalus' serene-looking head gives us no sense of all the demons teeming within – no emperor had so complex an interior life. How happy he was it is hard to say: he indulged his desires to the full, but never seemed remotely satisfied.

While Macrinus' position was steadily weakening, the surviving Julias had been building their powerbase. Cleverly, they drew on their family's Syrian background. Their father had been a famous priest, so they had Bassianus placed in the same role, in Syria's most important shrine. They renamed him after the god of the temple, 'Elagabalus'. In that role, and under that new name, he was revered throughout the whole of Syria, and well beyond, where this eastern cult had taken hold.

SPIN AND LIES

But the re-branding didn't stop there. The Julias concocted a fictional pedigree for Elagabalus, claiming that he had been born of an affair between Soaemias

A SYRIAN SUN GOD

The Julias' father, Julius Bassianus, had been the High Priest of Emesa's Temple of the Sun, which was one of Syria's most important shrines. Here, worshippers came to adore a wondrous black stone that had been sent down from heaven (a meteorite, we would call it now). Its jagged edges and points suggested the rays streaming out of the sun as traditionally depicted, so it was seen as a gift from that great giver of warmth and life.

El was a Semitic name for the one supreme deity, 'God' (and ultimately the root of the Arabic word *Allah*). *Baal* was the name for his Aramaean manifestation. Here, at his most important shrine, he was given the two names together and known to the Syrians as *El-Gabal*.

When the Romans settled in the region, many were drawn to this local cult. They identified the idea of the one high god *El* with the Greek word *Helio* for 'sun'. They had traditionally worshipped large numbers of gods, but if they had to imagine a single all-powerful deity it was natural for them to associate him with the sun. In his Roman form, then, this greatest of gods became known as *Heliogabalus* (or *Elegabalus*) *Sol Invictus*, which might be translated as 'God the Undefeated Sun'.

As Emperor, Elagabalus had a temple built in Rome, the *Elagabalium*, and had the meteorite-idol transported there from Emesa.

The cult of Elagabalus tapped into that of El, an ancient Semitic god still worshipped in the east.

and Caracalla. Not only was he the chosen one of God, then, but he was also the nearest thing that the murdered Emperor had had to an heir. By rights, then, Elagabalus should have the imperial throne, transmitted from Septimius Severus to his son Caracalla, then wrongfully usurped by Macrinus, the lowly born impostor.

To strengthen his supposed claim to the throne, Elagabalus changed his name afresh, this time to Marcus Aurelius Antoninus. These were the names that Caracalla had been given in his boyhood, so they cemented the seeming connection with Elagabalus' 'father'. Caracalla himself had been given them because they harked back to the last of the 'Good Emperors', Antoninus Pius and Marcus Aurelius, so one way or another they backed Elagabalus's claims of legitimacy.

> On 18 May 218 C.E., the Third Gallic Legion proclaimed Elagabalus Emperor at its camp in Raphana, in the north of modern Jordan.

If you boil it all down to essentials this was an extremely flimsy story, but the legions in the east were more than ready to be convinced. They were thoroughly disillusioned with Macrinus, who showed no signs of being able to bring them victory in war, which was really the first duty of any Emperor. On 18 May 218 C.E., the Third Gallic Legion proclaimed Elagabalus Emperor at its camp in Raphana, in the north of modern Jordan. Although Macrinus sent out an army to put the rebels down, it never even made it to the battlefield before the men mutinied and killed their commanding officers. The officers' heads were mounted on spikes and sent back to Antioch as a message to Macrinus. The troops then enlisted in the cause of Elagabalus.

Reinforced by these latest recruits, Elagabalus' men set out for Antioch to place their Emperor on the throne. Improbable as it may sound, they were led by Gannys, the boy's eunuch tutor. On 8 June, Macrinus marched what was left of his own army out to meet them. His support had been draining away in the intervening weeks. His force was badly defeated, and

although he fled in a messenger's disguise he was recaptured in Cappadoccia and put to death. His son, Diadumenianus, was at first given sanctuary by the Parthians, but afterwards executed as a gesture of friendship towards the new regime.

RELIGIOUS DIFFERENCES

And so, in his mid-teens, Elagabalus found himself ascending the imperial throne. His accession wasn't actually anything like as controversial as it should have been. Far from having elected him, Rome's Senate hadn't even been consulted. They didn't quibble about his enthronement, though. It seems they were only too happy to see some sort of stability restored after the uncertainty that had dogged Macrinus' reign.

But it wasn't long before people started having second thoughts about whether accepting this particular Emperor had been such a good idea. Even before they had seen him for themselves, while he was still making his journey to Rome, doubts were surfacing about his suitability for the role. His name itself seemed strange and exotic. There was no more talk of 'Marcus Aurelius Antoninus' now. It was made clear that he was going to reign as Elagabalus. To prepare people for his coming, his mother sent a full-length portrait of the new Emperor in his priestly robes, and ordered that it be hung from the ceiling of the Senate House, high above the statue of Victoria. By tradition, before each gathering, sacrifices were offered to the goddess of Victory. Now it would seem as if they were being offered to Elagabalus.

That wasn't all. In his exotic oriental outfit Elagabalus didn't resemble the Romans idea of what an Emperor should look like. And the news from the east was by no means reassuring. The imperial party had settled down to wait out the winter in Bithynia, northwestern Turkey, and those with him were growing seriously alarmed. Elagabalus was really serious about his priesthood. He performed mystic rites and went into strange religious ecstasies. It all seemed alien and downright weird.

Rather than preparing the way for her son, then, Julia Soaemias had actually only succeeded in

Elagabalus, in full regalia and robes, leads an act of worship in the Temple of the Sun. As if his lifestyle were not exotic enough, Elagabalus' religious observances – rooted in Syrian traditions – came as a deep shock to the priests and citizenry of Rome.

ensuring that the Romans were prejudiced against him from the start.

LUXURY GONE MAD

But these religious differences were the least of the Romans' problems with Elagabalus, whose lifestyle was outrageous in its extravagance. Augustus and Livia had made a point of living simple, austere lives in keeping with the values of Republican Rome. Those days were long gone by now, but even so, to the astonishment of the people of Rome, Elagabalus' lust for luxury seemed not so much excessive as insane.

He had his banqueting hall, his private chambers and even the porticoes in which he walked carpeted with the petals of violets, lilies and hyacinths. He had a special ceiling installed, which would release a shower of petals on the diners below. In one famous incident, several of his darlings were killed when the flowers fell so thickly that they were smothered.

The Emperor was always on the lookout for a novelty, and the perversity of his whims took the Romans' breath away. Once, when he was staying in a villa deep in the country during the heat of the summer, he was seized by the impulse to have a mountain of snow built in the garden there. It had to

> In one famous incident, several of Elagabalus's darlings were killed when the flowers fell so thickly that they were smothered.

be brought by the cartload all the way from the Alpine heights, but nothing would persuade Elagabalus that this wasn't a fabulous scheme.

He wouldn't swim in a pool that hadn't first been made fragrant with saffron, rosewater or some other scent. He had his couches covered with gold leaf, that is, when they weren't actually made of solid silver. But he couldn't rest comfortably on them unless the

'The Roses of Heliogabalus', as imagined by a nineteenth-century artist: the idea that one might drown in beauty, die in an excess of pleasure, appealed to the aesthetic movement of that time – as it appears to have appealed to the Emperor himself.

cushions had been stuffed with rabbit fur or the soft down taken from the underside of partridge's wings. He had golden chamber pots made for his own use, and his urinals were made of onyx. He would never wear anything – shoes, clothing, even jewels – more than once. Wives apart, he never slept with a woman a second time.

A PICKY EATER

Only the choicest delicacies, such as peacock tongues and the combs of cockerels, cruelly cut away from the heads of living fowl, would do for Elagabalus. He ate mullet's guts, camel heels, the heads of tropical parrots and the brains of flamingos, and the stranger and more difficult to find the food, the better he liked it. On the same principle he refused to eat fish or seafood when he was near the coast, but insisted on eating nothing else when he was far inland. More conventional foods could only be made sufficiently exquisite for him to eat by being sprinkled with tiny pearls or flakes of gold, onyx or amber. Or he might have fish cooked in a blue sauce so that it seemed it was still swimming in seawater.

He had strange habits when it came to food. One day he would eat only pheasant; another only pork. On yet another day it had to be ostrich or some special kind of fish. One day he might insist on having only

His imperial bust represents Elagabalus as the Roman establishment would have liked to see him: generally, though, he did not give them the chance. The Emperor's public face was pretty much as decadent as his private one, so little trouble did he take to be discreet.

food that was green; another day, it would have to be yellow or some other shade. His pets dined hardly less exquisitely than he did. His dogs were given goose livers, and he had grapes brought all the way from Syria for his horses.

HAIR-RAISING HILARITY

At times his eccentricity shaded over into something more disturbing, and there was definitely a sadistic edge to his sense of fun. Once, for example, he thought it would be a great joke to release hundreds of snakes into the crowd that had assembled for the public games. Many were seriously hurt, whether by the snakes themselves or after falling or being crushed in the resulting panic. On more than one occasion, he strapped a young beloved to a water wheel to enjoy the sight of him spinning beneath the surface, then coming up spluttering.

So, when a friend got drunk in his company, he thought it a great laugh to lock him in the cage of one of the private menagerie he maintained – that of

ECCENTRIC ENTERTAINMENTS

When he was in the mood to host a party, Elagabalus' generosity knew no bounds. In fact, it didn't seem to show much reason because he entertained on a dementedly lavish scale. A guest was likely to leave a banquet of his with a gift from his host that might be anything from a four-horse chariot through a eunuch slave to a hundred pounds in silver.

His chefs and confectioners could work miracles, but his menus were sometimes designed to astound rather than to please. Once, for example, he had his chefs serve vast platters of beautifully prepared mice and weasels. At another 'feast', his chosen guests found themselves being offered every kind of delicacy, but made of glass.

On another evening, stunning pictures of food were served while the guests went hungry.

It amused him to play games with his guest list. He would invite all bald men, all one-eyed men, all fat men, and so on, and enjoy their surprise as the 'theme' of the evening sank in. Once he gave a banquet at which each course in turn was served in the house of a different one of his guests, even though they came from very far-flung parts of the city. That meal ended up going on all through the night and right into the next day. And he did not forget the people in his bounty. Not content with sponsoring the usual shows and spectacles, he staged a mock sea battle on a canal that had been filled with wine.

DRIVING OBSESSION

There was often an air of eccentricity about Elagabalus' public appearances, as when he paraded through the capital in a chariot drawn by camels. On another occasion it was elephants. This stunt was only practicable because he had several historic tombs demolished in advance. Contemporary commentators also describe him proudly promenading in a chariot pulled variously by lions, tigers, stags and enormous dogs.

Chariot driving, the more unconventional the better, seems to have been something of an obsession with the adolescent Emperor. He would drive into his banqueting hall so as to make a suitably spectacular entrance. Sometimes, cracking his whip and yelling delightedly, he would appear before his astonished guests in a chariot drawn by beautiful naked women.

It went without saying that Elagabalus's chariots were magnificent creations made of gold and encrusted with the richest jewels. It is reported that he refused to drive a vehicle made merely of silver or ivory.

a bear or leopard, for example. The poor man would wake next morning not just hungover, but in abject terror. Only slowly would he realize what Elagabalus had known all along: all his animals were absolutely tame.

WIVES AND RELIGION

In 219 C.E., Elagabalus married Julia Cornelia Paula, a young woman famous for her elegance and beauty, and another member of the Romano-Syrian elite. Not much else is known about her. In any case, she was set aside the following year so that Elagabalus could make a more controversial match. As a consul's daughter,

The Vestal Virgins were a sacred institution, as old as Rome itself: nowhere did Elagabalus' lack of sensitivity and political savvy come through more clearly or more damagingly than in his decision to marry a member of this ancient sisterhood.

Aquilia Severa would have seemed an entirely appropriate choice as an emperor's bride. There was just one problem. She was a vestal virgin. The purity of these priestesses of Vesta, goddess of the hearth, was seen as being vital to the wellbeing of Rome, – not just its morals but also its actual security.

Hence the symbolic importance of this marriage was immense – and immensely damaging, as far as the Romans were concerned. Elagabalus saw it completely differently. For him, it represented a fusion of the

> He made himself up like a woman, plucking the hair from his body and wearing wigs and feminine gowns before going into the lowest and sleaziest of the city's dives to sell his body as a common prostitute.

eastern sun cult he represented with the ancestral religion of the Romans. So this was a spiritual marriage between himself as El-Gabal and Aquilia Severa as embodiment of Vesta and all her values. It may have sounded reasonable to the Emperor, but to the Romans it seemed that he was debauching the very mark of distinction of their city.

So great was the public outrage that Elagabalus' grandmother Julia Maesa stepped in. She made him divorce Aquilia Severa and marry another woman in July 221 C.E. Annia Faustina could hardly have been improved on as a bride. As a great-granddaughter of the Emperor Marcus Aurelius, she had the approval of everyone in Rome.

Everyone except Elagabalus, that is. By the end of the year he had divorced Annia Faustina and re-created his spiritual match with Aquilia Severa.

ELAGABALUS THE AMBIGUOUS

His relationship with his second and fourth wife may genuinely have been more about symbolism than sex. Elagabalus' religious feelings, like everything else about him, were extravagant, but they seem to have been sincere. But there's also any amount of evidence to suggest that his real romantic and sexual passions were

directed not at women, but men. The only reason he had sex with women at all, one of his contemporaries suggests, was so that he could learn from them how better to satisfy his male lovers.

The great love of his life was a charioteer from Caria, southwestern Turkey. His name was Hierocles. The story went that they had met by chance when, racing before the Emperor one day, the youth had been thrown from his chariot and had landed at Elagabalus' feet. Hierocles had been born a slave, of course, but to Elagabalus' mind he was the most important man on earth. 'I am thrilled to be Hierocles' mistress, his wife, his queen,' he said. They went through a form of marriage, which the Emperor at least took entirely seriously. Elagabalus even tried to name his beloved 'Caesar' and make him his successor, but again Julia Maesa intervened to save him from himself. She was growing increasingly alarmed at the publicity Elagabalus was getting for his sexual escapades, publicity he was making no attempt to shun.

He made himself up like a woman, plucking the hair from his body and wearing wigs and feminine gowns before going into the lowest and sleaziest of the city's dives to sell his body as a common prostitute. He would have his men raid a brothel and drive the women out, but only so that he could offer his services in their place. He even played the prostitute in the imperial palace. He would stand, half-hidden by a hanging, and look out languorously, invitingly, calling seductively to any man who passed.

A QUESTION OF IDENTITY

After so many emperors and so many scandals, it took a lot to shock the Romans, but it's safe to say that Elagabalus' activities left them reeling. That was never going to sway the Emperor, who had much more than simply a streak of mischief. He enjoyed offending pieties for the fun of it.

On one occasion, he sent his men out to go through all the city's brothels, taverns and roadhouses, and round up all the women they could find. Parties

Annia Faustina was Elagabalus' third wife, forced on him by his mother in response to the outcry stirred up by his second, disastrous marriage. All approved this new match – with the crucial exception of the Emperor himself, who quickly divorced Faustina and took up with Aquilia Severa once again.

A LIMP PERFORMANCE

The only real threat to Hierocles in the Emperor's affections seems to have been a certain Aurelius Zoticus, who came from Smyrna. He was famed as an athlete, both actual and sexual, and he was celebrated for his physical beauty. But his chief attraction by quite some way was his male member. All who had seen it said no one else's even came close in size.

Elagabalus was naturally desperate to meet this living legend and to make the acquaintance of this extraordinary organ. It was easily enough arranged. The Emperor had Zoticus seized at a sports meeting where he was competing, and brought before him at the imperial palace. Flashing his most feminine glances at his guest, Elagabalus was disconcerted when the athlete hailed him as 'my Lord'. 'Do not call me that,' Elagabalus reprimanded him. 'I am your Lady.'

These greetings over, Elagabalus had the new guest brought to him in his bath. Once Zoticus was disrobed, Elagabalus saw that there had been no exaggeration. As they lounged together in the relaxing water, attendants brought snacks and drinks. Elagabalus couldn't get enough of his new friend. He wrapped himself around him in the bath, then afterwards on the couch. But Hierocles had friends among the Emperor's cupbearers, and they had slipped something into Zoticus' wine. Despite strenuous efforts, he was unable to achieve an erection. Even more strenuous and increasingly panic-stricken efforts ensued, for it became clearer and clearer as the night went on that the frustrated Emperor didn't view Zoticus's plight with sympathy. Zoticus feared for his life. In the end, he escaped with exile. Elagabalus had him hounded from the palace, from the city of Rome and from Italy.

combed through all the darkest and dirtiest streets and alleys, and the arcades around the amphitheatres, until all the capital's prostitutes had been caught. Then, having herded them together in a vast arena, he addressed them in a ringing oration, a parody of the speech the general gives when rallying the troops. Dressed and made up as if he were one of their company, he called them his 'comrades', and thanked them for their vital contribution, the heroic services they had performed for the glory of Rome. He then went on to discourse to them on his preferred sexual activities and positions, before dismissing them with gold coins, as though this were a soldiers' *donativum*. Another day, he had Rome's male prostitutes brought together for a similar gathering. This time, though, he appeared as a young catamite, presenting his bare buttocks suggestively to the crowd.

But there seems to have been a more serious side to Elagabalus' experiments in femininity. At some level he appears to have been what we would call 'transexual', in that he genuinely wanted to be a woman. His interests were not limited to sexual role-playing, however. He would also pursue non-sexual activities associated with women, such as sewing and

From Ephesos, the relief of a footprint with a woman's head: taken together these are believed to be a sign alerting citizens to a nearby brothel. Elagabalus appears to have had a strange fascination with the world of prostitution – even participating himself in his transvestite guise.

weaving, for example. And even his sexual interests seem to have gone some way beyond the merely frivolous. The contemporary historian Dio Cassius reports that Elagabalus called in all the finest physicians and surgeons of his day, promising them vast sums if they could devise an operation that might give him a vagina.

LOSING THE LEGIONS

It was all very well for Elagabalus to try to explore his sexuality and his gender, but he was supposed to be the ruler of the Roman Empire. And the Empire was, when all was said and done, a military enterprise. The Emperor would stand or fall by the quality of his relationship with his soldiers, which, in Elagabalus' case, wasn't good. It hadn't been from early on, the first doubts starting to surface even before he reached Rome as the new Emperor, while he and his army

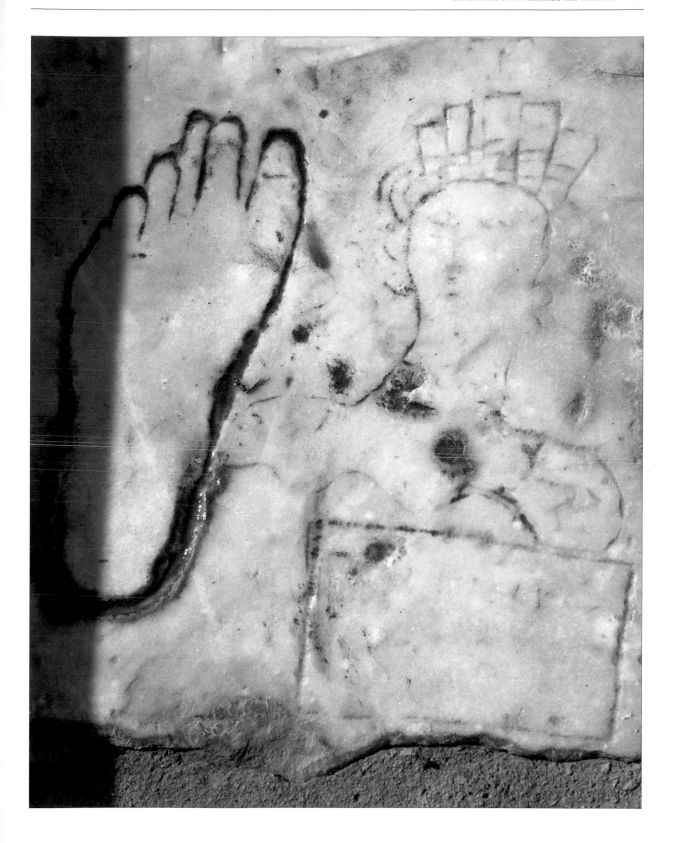

With Elagabalus' reign all too evidently spiralling out of control, Alexander Severus seemed to represent the last chance for the Severan Dynasty. He had much more natural authority: here, on campaign in Mesopotamia, he persuades a mutinous legion to lay down its arms.

were overwintering in Bithynia at the end of 218 C.E. His troops couldn't work out which they found more creepy: his religious or his sexual obsessions.

Did it show impressive honesty that Elagabalus never attempted to hide these things, or was it just a mark of outrageous arrogance on his part? In the end it didn't matter. The legionaries who had put him on the throne were straightforward, rough-and-ready Romans, and they were growing increasingly uncomfortable with the way their Emperor was behaving.

As ever, it was Julia Maesa who saw the way things were heading and decided to intervene. She realized that Elagabalus would have to go. It was no use

asking her daughter, the Emperor's mother, Julia Soaemias, to take action. She had encouraged her son in his religious eccentricities. Instead, she talked with her other daughter, Julia Mamaea, and they started grooming her young son, Alexander Severus, for the succession.

Julia Maesa nagged and bullied Elagabalus into naming his 13-year-old cousin as his successor. In 221 C.E., the boy was appointed his consul and, effectively, co-ruler. A year later, though, the Emperor thought better of this arrangement. It was only too obvious that Alexander Severus was proving more popular than Elagabalus himself was, and not just with their grandmother, but with the troops as well.

ALL UNRAVELS

Elagabaus sensed that they were using the boy as a means of easing him out. Unfortunately, his attempts to prevent this only brought it on. He tried to organize the boy's assassination, but this was unsuccessful because loyal troops guarded him carefully. Eventually, in a fit of temper, Elagabalus dismissed his cousin and stripped him of all his offices and rank. This enraged the legions and the Praetorian Guard.

The Emperor now spread a story that Alexander Severus was seriously ill. He was hoping to test the troops' reaction to the news. He got more than he bargained for. In a fury, they demanded that he produce the boy so they could see that he hadn't been done away with. Elagabalus and his mother, Julia Soaemias, called a meeting, at which Alexander Severus was presented before the men, but this didn't call forth the gratitude that the Emperor had hoped. Instead, the assembled ranks made it all too clear how much they loved the boy and how much they despised the Emperor himself.

Piqued by this display, Elagabalus gave orders that those who had shown disrespect to him should be arrested and executed. The command proved to be his

death warrant. Massing menacingly around the podium on which he and his mother were standing, the men prepared to drag them down and kill them. Elagabalus tried to conceal himself in a large chest, hoping his attendants might be able to spirit him away, but it was hopeless. He was dragged out of his hiding place.

His mother clung to him as the men attacked, but both were savagely done to death. They were beheaded and their bodies were stripped naked, before being dragged in bloody triumph through the streets, then dumped into the Tiber. Known supporters of Elagabalus, including his beloved Hierocles, were hunted down and killed in the hours that followed.

Elagabalus' attempts to organize Alexander Severus' death proved a step too far for a long-suffering military establishment – and for the common soldiery, who now turned on their Emperor and his mother. Both were killed, clearing Alexander Severus' path to the throne: he was very much the soldier's choice.

EPILOGUE

After Elagabalus, just about any emperor would have been an improvement. And so it proved, but events were conspiring against the Empire. A succession of rulers sought to stem the slow diminution of power and prestige, but Rome was now in terminal decline.

Elagabalus' death had been a bloody farce. It had been horrific and undignified. Two and a half centuries after the office of Emperor had been established by Augustus, it had all come to a transvestite teenager cowering in a wooden chest. Not that the majority of his predecessors had been so spectacularly impressive. It's hard to think of Caligula or Nero as *patres patriae* ('fathers of their fatherland'). Indeed, all the emperors had fallen short of the majestic authority their various titles seemed to

Maximus Thrax, who reigned from 235 c.e., was the first of the so-called 'Barracks Emperors' (the second, Aurelian, is represented on the coin above). With the Empire increasingly fighting for survival, the army became all-important: the tendency was for the military tail to wag the governmental dog.

suggest. They had been mere human beings, and often desperately damaged ones.

Outrageous as they were, Elagabalus' faults had hardly been the worst Rome had seen. The problem was that it was beginning to matter more. With Rome inexorably on the rise, the personal foibles of the man at the top had hardly signified. Now, though, its Empire was as vulnerable as it was vast. Rome's territories now extended over almost 6 million square kilometres (2.3 million square miles). That meant keeping many hundreds of subject peoples in their place. Thousands of miles of frontier had to be policed and protected at a time when, beyond the boundaries of the Roman world, things were changing, new powers coming to the fore.

Later historians would blame the decline of Rome on everything from decadence to Christianity, from too

THE DENARIUS DEBASED

Today, governments and central banks in difficulties print too much money, but paper currency didn't exist in Roman times. Instead, the Romans relied on their coinage. The mighty denarius, almost pure silver, had been the economic underpinning of the *Pax Romana*.

Unfortunately, Emperors from Domitian on had found the minting of more and more coins the perfect way of fulfilling their rash promises. Or, at least, it had appeared to be the perfect way. The reality was that they didn't have enough silver to create coinage of the requisite material value. The temptation, then, was to mix in less prestigious metals so that the same coin could be made more cheaply. The trouble was, of course, that it wasn't really the same, and people knew it.

Recognizing that the real worth of the denarius had slipped, farmers, tradesmen and merchants responded by raising prices. The result, inevitably, was galloping inflation. By the time Diocletian came to the throne, few wanted to have anything to do with the Roman currency, and the vast majority of trade was conducted by means of barter.

Diocletian is depicted on what was now a currency debased. Values had slumped by the time of his accession in 284 C.E. As far as his critics were concerned, he further diluted Roman power by dividing up the Empire – although this arguably helped to stave off its inevitable collapse.

much partying to too much praying. In truth, an Empire that could grow in leaps and bounds even through the reigns of Caligula and Nero was hardly going to be brought crashing down by the odd orgy. Neither, on the other hand, was there any appreciable sign that the Romans were embracing what was seen as a slightly peculiar sect of Judaism. There was certainly no indication that they were forsaking the ways of conquest for Jesus and His path of peace.

What is clear is that the Empire had grown to such a size that it was facing an ever-present problem of being overstretched. Hadrian had recognized this as long ago as the 130s C.E.; hence his attempts to fortify key frontiers. But it was hard to hold the line, especially when so many of the Empire's troops were now recruited from the subject nations and felt no special attachment to Italy or Rome.

At the time of Elagabalus' death, the Empire was beset by difficulties extending east and west. In

Europe, Germanic tribes along the frontier were growing restless. In Asia, meanwhile, the Parthian Empire was finally foundering, but only to give way to the power of Persia's Sassanid kings. Rome had never been more sorely in need of authoritative leadership.

ALEXANDER ADRIFT

There was a man's job to be done, but circumstances had sent another boy. Alexander Severus was only 14 years old. As far as we can tell, he was well meaning, but never really very forceful. He just wasn't what the Empire needed at this time. His mother, Julia Mamaea, had enough personality for two. Like her aunt Julia Domna, she was a warrior-woman, going

Philip the Arab, as represented in what remains of a statue found in Corsica. The son of a sheikh from Syria, his reign lasted just five years, from 244 until 249 C.E., though this was a respectable term by the standards of the time.

with the new Emperor on campaign. But her
interfering ways only alienated the legions – most
especially, her attempts to cut back on their bonuses.

In the event, the army managed to hold back the
Sassanid advance, but at the cost of crumbling morale
and mounting discontent. In the west, though, the
Germanic tribes were by now freely raiding and
plundering northern and eastern Gaul. Alexander was
reduced to paying the invaders off. What little
authority he had possessed as Emperor was fatally
compromised by this concession. In 235 C.E., there
was a military mutiny, and Alexander and his mother
were both assassinated.

THE IMPERIAL CRISIS

Alexander's replacement, Gaius Julius Verus Maximinus,
was known as Maximinus Thrax because of his origins
in Thrace, to the northeast of Greece. This made him
the first barbarian Emperor ever. Not only was he an
outsider, but he had never even been to Rome. Nor
would he go there through the entirety of his reign. His
term at the top wasn't to be a long one, though.
Maximinus' reign represented another 'first' because he
began the succession of 'Barracks Emperors'.

Rome had always been a military power; in fact, it
had always had a tendency towards out-and-out
militarism, emphasizing soldierly values at the expense
of others. Now, though, the world's greatest empire
became a politically bankrupt state ruled by one tin-
pot military dictator after another for a generation. The
priorities of the new regime were made explicitly clear
by Maximinus Thrax's one great policy 'achievement':
the doubling of soldiers' pay throughout the Empire.
This would have been great for the legionaries if there
had been any way the Empire could sustain it. But of
course it couldn't begin to. This was economic policy
at its most infantile.

The result was crisis – first economic, then political.
In April 238 C.E., Maximinus Thrax was assassinated.
Another military commander, the aged Gordian I, who
ruled alongside his son Gordian II, replaced him. They
lasted just over a month before Maximinus' supporters
overthrew them, but the Senate felt obliged to keep faith

**The Sack of Rome by the Visigoths in 410 C.E. was the ultimate
humiliation for what had been the ancient world's pre-eminent
power. The abilities of its rulers scarcely seemed to matter now:
time was running out fast for the Roman Empire.**

with the Gordians. Pupienus and Balbinus came to the throne, but only as caretakers keeping it for Gordian I's grandson Gordian III. As he ascended the throne in his own right on 29 July, that made 238 C.E. the 'Year of Six Emperors', which was a record, even by the standards of the 'Imperial Crisis'.

In fact, over the next 25 years or so, few emperors were going to last for more than a couple of years. One of the exceptions, however, was Gordian III's successor, Philip the Arab. Born in southeastern Syria, he was the son of an Arab sheikh who had been given citizenship in return for his services to Rome. Enthroned in 244 C.E. he was overthrown in 249 C.E. by Decius, a rival commander whose powerbase lay among the armies on the Danube and in the Balkans. Trebonianus Gallus, who in his turn was overthrown in 253 C.E. by Aemilianus, toppled Decius in 251 C.E. It went without saying that both men were assassinated.

> The imperial succession struggled on, but Rome was now only too obviously a power in terminal decline.

And so it went on. The world's greatest empire, ungovernable and more or less completely bankrupt, was now a complete basket case. The habit of overthrowing emperors had become ingrained, meaning that each new ruler was no more powerful than the particular body of troops who had backed him. There were always other groups trying to promote their man for their particular advantage. And as the first thing each emperor did on coming to power was to try to buy the troops' support with increases in pay, the Empire's economic plight grew worse and worse.

DIOCLETIAN DOMINANT
It seemed like more of the same when, on 20 November 284 C.E., the Emperor Diocletian came to the throne. But he was to stay in power for more than 20 years. He

Justinian I has gone down in history as the 'Last Roman', but he was also the first great emperor of Byzantium. Greek-speaking and Christian, this new empire marked a distinct departure, but it kept alive many of the achievements of ancient Rome.

saved the Empire, although you could easily argue that he did so only by destroying it. He was the most dictatorial emperor yet in his way of ruling, but he was prepared to share power to some extent. He it was who established the Tetrarchy ('Rule of Four'). He realized that no single individual could possibly control so vast a realm, with all its internal tensions and external threats, and so he shared out power with three of his comrades. He also divided the Empire down the middle, into eastern and western realms. This made sense, but it was coming to seem like it was no longer the Roman Empire. Rome itself was marooned in the more impoverished, western part.

THE EMPIRE IMPLODES
The Empire was already struggling to withstand the impact of raids from the Germanic tribes. As the fourth century wore on, pressure started building in the east. Far out in the Central Asian steppe, war-like nomadic tribes were on the move, pushing westward to find fresh pastures for their livestock, and fresh opportunities for plunder. Peoples such as the Huns, ferocious fighters and ruthless raiders, were fearsome in themselves. But their indirect impact was every bit as important. As they pushed west, the peoples in their path were displaced and forced to move before them. They were more or less impelled to spill across the frontiers of the Roman Empire. Wave after wave of barbarian invaders, such as the Goths and Vandals and various other tribes, now irrupted into the Roman Empire.

Rome itself was sacked by the Visigoths in 410 C.E., then again by the Vandals 45 years later. The imperial succession struggled on, but Rome was now only too obviously a power in terminal decline. The end came in the 'reign' of Romulus Augustus in 476 C.E. He was only 12 or so when he was enthroned, and he had been in office for just under a year when he was forced to renounce his title by Odoacer, a Germanic chief.

Augustus and Vespasian would have disdained such a man as a brutish barbarian. It was ignominious that the Emperor had to take his orders. And yet, it was a fitting final end for a Roman Empire brought lower and lower through the reigns of such a motley crew of emperors.

In the east, the Empire endured, reinventing itself as the civilization of Byzantium. In the west, though, chaos and anarchy ensued. The 'dark history' of the Roman Emperors had ended, perhaps inevitably, in what we nowadays think of as the 'Dark Ages'.

INDEX

PICTURE CREDITS